A N E N T
MICHAEL J

THE LIFE & TIMES

of

MICHAEL J. RODDEN

in

NORTHERN ONTARIO

in his own words

Edited by Peter Handley

Published by
Highway Book Shop
Cobalt, Ontario
P0J 1C0

Anent Michael J
The Life & Times of Michael J. Rodden
in Northern Ontario, in his own words

ISBN 0-88954-410-7

Canadian Cataloguing in Publication Data

Rodden, Michael J., 1891-1978
    Anent Michael J.: the life & times of Michael J. Rodden in
Northern Ontario in his own words

ISBN 0-88954-410-7

1. Rodden, Michael J., 1891-1978. 2. Ontario, Northern –
Anecdotes. 3. Athletes – Canada – Biography. 4. Sportswriters
– Canada – Biography.
I. Handley, Peter, 1933-   . II. Title.
GV697.R63A3 1999   796'.092   C99-930924-2

Cover photo courtesy of Queen's University Archives and Dana Rodden
Inside front photo courtesy of Queen's University Archives

TABLE OF CONTENTS

Editor's Comments

Mike Rodden was a true original. As the old expression has it, *"They broke the mould when he was born."* You will discover the truth of that statement as you read the pages of this little book.

Late in life Mike Rodden decided to put all his many stories together and he carefully crafted his autobiography, all 500 pages of it. He couldn't interest a publisher before he died in 1978 at age 87. The manuscript, which had been given to former football star Frank Cosentino, ended up in the hands of long time journalist Bill Fitsell in Kingston, home of the International Hockey Hall of Fame.

Mike Rodden was a friend of mine as I grew up in the Limestone City, playing baseball and getting involved in the media. He helped teach me to score ball games and often regaled me with stories as I sat next to him in the Kingston Memorial Centre pressbox as we covered Senior hockey games together – Mike for the Kingston Whig Standard. and me for CKWS radio.

When I was transferred to North Bay in early 1958, Mike made a point of telling me, via letters, all about his birthplace – Mattawa, and as we kept in touch over the next few years, he described 'hookstag' and the rapids and many of the things you will read about in the following pages.

After Mike's passing in '78, I began to wonder what had happened to his reminiscences. Finally, through the help of old friend Don Boswell, who worked with Rodden at the Whig for many years, I was put in touch with Bill Fitsell.

My idea was to put together a book of Mike's life in Mattawa and Northern Ontario, and make it available to visitors to his home town, which has named its artificial ice surface, the Mike Rodden Arena. Fitsell pulled out the many chapters of Mike's story that involved Northern Ontario and you hold the result in your hands.

Mike Rodden was truly an unforgettable character and he had an unforgettable character just as he had an unforgettable writing style. He was the master of the florid – they used to call it 'purple prose' – but he was also the master of facts and the teller of what seemed like tall tales – but stories that always could be borne out by research (well – almost always).

Back in 1978, I was writing a column for North Bay Living called "Pickin 'em up & Puttin 'em down". On his passing, I wrote two episodes about Mike – here is a portion of one of them – and it is a typical Rodden Story.

"In the early forties the war was on, but that didn't stop sports – baseball, hockey, football et al went on – at a reduced rate but it went on.

Many athletes were in the armed forces and some of them were able to keep up some form of athletic endeavour. I can recall my dad taking me to see Syl Apps (Sr.) and Adam Brown playing hockey for a couple of army teams at the old Jock Harty Arena in Kingston.

About the same time various U.S. military baseball teams were formed and they would play exhibition games. One of them ventured across the border into Canada and played against a local team in Kingston – which at the time had some pretty fine ball players. The score-keeper received a lot of abuse after the game because he didn't give four errors to the U.S. second baseman; as he related the story to me many years later the scorekeeper remarked – "That second baseman was the only really good ball player out there – he played each of the balls in question properly but the infield at the Cricket Field was in pretty poor shape that day and bad hops were the order of the day and as a result I didn't call errors – I had a lot of static thrown at me – but that wasn't unusual!"

Two footnotes to that story – the second baseman was Red Schoendienst and he went on to become an all time great with the St. Louis Cardinals after the war. The scorekeeper, of course, was Mike

Rodden of Mattawa who died last week after 87 years of vibrant life that saw him become one of this country's most fabulous sports figures.

His achievements? Where to begin is the problem – he spent fifty odd years in sports, first as a player in hockey, lacrosse, baseball, football, hookstag, and canoeing, and then as a coach and referee and finally as a sportswriter and columnist.

He became the first Canadian to be named to two Sports Halls of Fame – Hockey in '62 and Football in 1964. He coached teams to 27 different titles including Grey Cups with Hamilton in '28 and '29; attending Ottawa U and then Queen's he won 15 sports letters at the latter (still a school record); he played hockey at Queen's, Haileybury and Toronto St. Pats and coached the sport for at least five schools; won Intercollegiate All Star football honours at four different positions; refereed 2,864 hockey games including an amazing 1,187 in the NHL in 13 years. He was with the Toronto Globe for 18 years – eight as Editor and during that time was official scorer for Leaf International League games. He was Sports Editor at the Kingston Whig Standard for 15 years... he had an astute eye for talent and recommended some 32 players who made the NHL – Nels Stewart, Toe Blake, Butch Keeling and Hap Emms among them... I could go on.

I first met Mike in the late forties when I was writing High School sports; when I was playing Juvenile and Junior Baseball and also scoring games he gave me a number of tips – and that story about Schoendienst was one of them.

I have a number of sharp edged memories of Michael J. - sitting at the end of a wooden players bench at the Cricket Field in Kingston, clad in a rumpled striped brown suit, cigarette dripping grey ash down his vest, carefully scoring every happening on the diamond in a six by three pad. Mike always had a jacket pocket full of little red and blue pencils sharpened like needles, and he marked the home team in red and the visitors in blue (or vice versa), a tactic he also used when covering Queen's Intercollegiate football matches."

As you will find when you read this book, Rodden was never inclined to pull his punches (and he threw a few too as you will discover). It didn't matter if he was talking to the President of the NHL, a pompous team owner or an all star player – he spoke, and wrote, the truth as he saw it – and he saw a lot!

"I drank my way through three fortunes" he told me one night when we were covering a senior hockey match together, "but Millie stuck with me through everything." Millie and Mike were married for 63 years and Rodden used to beam with pride when he would say, "I married the prettiest girl at Queen's" and then he'd wink roguishly. I hope you enjoy the following pages. They vibrantly tell the story of an earlier time here in northeastern Ontario. A time when a young man's mettle was forged on various playing fields, in looming black-green forests, on foam whipped rivers, in mining camps, on mud soaked portages, in hideous smoke and flame and in rustic bar-rooms in equally rustic hotels. Who would have guessed that that young man who grew up playing hookstag, running rapids and fighting forest fires would develop into one of Canada's most storied coaches, referees and writers.

Peter Handley
Editor

Anent Our Title

Mike Rodden had a good command of the English language and he developed a writing style that could be termed a form of "purple prose", to use an oldtime expression. He also delighted in the use of somewhat quaint expressions, terms from another time. For example, if a hockey player received a penalty Mike would quite often write that he spent the next two minutes "in durance vile" (the penalty box).

Another favourite word in the Rodden lexicon was "anent". He would preface a paragraph concerning a particular player or event with – "anent the great Gordon 'Duke' Keats" or "anent the Black Sox scandal" as examples.

According to the Oxford Universal Dictionary the word, or a form of it, goes back prior to the 12th century and is classed as falling within the Old English period. One of the meanings of the word is "in respect or reference to, concerning," which apparently comes from Scottish use and was picked up by English writers around 1450.

So our title, using one of Mike's favourite words, simply means – "concerning" Michael J.

A Cautionary Note

The stories, thoughts, descriptions of people, places and events as written herein, are those of Michael J. Rodden himself, and do not reflect the views of his surviving relatives or the editor or publisher.

Some of the terms used and ideas expressed were commonplace when M.J.R. was growing up and should be viewed in that context.

Thank You Very Much

Without the help, co-operation and good wishes of a number of people, this little volume would never have been printed. The manuscript was found through the help of Don Boswell and put in our hands through the good graces of Bill Fitsell. Permission to use the material was given by Michael's grandchildren – Dana, Mark, Michael and Remy Rodden and Lia Argo.

Dana was also kind enough to provide many of the pictures used in the book, with the others coming from the Queen's Archives.

My wife, Pamela, undertook the mammoth task of re-typing the oft corrected manuscript – a job she completed in her usual good humour. Daughter Mairi Phillips also did some typing during a welcome visit home. Son Peter took the material and designed and produced the book on his Mac and then Doug Pollard of the famed Highway Book Shop in Cobalt, agreed to publish.

I would also like to extend my appreciation to Bill Silver, Bob Surtees and Sandro Orlando for their help and advice.

My sincere thanks to all of you for helping keep alive the memory and the words of a most unusual man.

pfh

MICHAEL J. RODDEN
A Biographical Sketch
Courtesy of Queen's University Archives

The first man in Canada to be named to both the Canadian Hockey Hall of Fame and the Canadian Football Hall of Fame, Michael James (Mike) Rodden (1891-1978), of the Class of Arts 1914 Queen's University, has earned recognition as one of the most outstanding sports personalities ever produced in Canada.

Mike was elected to the Hockey Hall of Fame in 1962 on the strength of his contribution to the sport as a referee – in all he officiated in 2,864 games, 1,187 of which were in the National Hockey League where he spent 13 years. He was named to the Football Hall of Fame in December, 1964, largely for his notable record as a coach – 27 championship football teams in various leagues.

Mr. Rodden's participation in sport covers more than half a century, first as a player in hockey, baseball, lacrosse, and football, then as a coach and referee and finally as a sports editor and columnist. Each of these endeavours could have been a career in itself and for three years he actually held down three jobs one of which would have been full-time employment for an average man: coach of the Hamilton Tigers – Grey Cup Winners in 1928 and again in 1929; referee in the National Hockey League, the International League, the Ontario Hockey Association, and other organizations – he refereed as many as sixteen games in a week; and was then sports editor of the Toronto Globe.

Mike was born in Mattawa, Ontario on April 24, 1891 where, among other things, he established numerous Northern Ontario records as a canoeist. From Mattawa he went to the University of Ottawa where he added football to his endeavours, and as the lightweight and welterweight boxing champion. He took part in the

Porcupine gold rush late in 1909 and served as a fire ranger and game warden for seven years. He entered Queen's in 1910, and when he left four years later he had won fifteen letters in football and hockey, still a record at the university. In football he made the allstar team four years in a row and at different positions each year; centre, tackle, flying wing and end. He also had the distinction of playing on the last Queen's hockey team to win an Intercollegiate Union senior championship, in 1914.

After university he played hockey in Haileybury in 1915 and with Toronto St. Patricks in 1917-1918. His coaching brought him many honours with De La Salle, Toronto St. Mary's, St. Patrick's (later Toronto Maple Leafs), University of Toronto Schools, Osgoode Hall, Argonaut Seniors, St. Andrew's College and the Belleville Senior B's. In 1921-1922 an all-time record was established when two of his teams, St. Andrew's and St. Mary's, clashed in the Ontario Hockey Association junior semi-finals. As a coach or scout he developed or sent thirty-two players to the National Hockey League, another record.

As a football coach his record was equally notable. Among his twenty-seven championships were the Toronto Argonauts, for whom he played as well, in 1920; Parkdale Canoe Club, unbeaten O.R.F.U. senior champions in 1921 and 1922; Hamilton Tigers, Big Four champions from 1927 to 1930 and Grey Cup winners in 1928 and 1929. From 1921 to 1938 he coached at the University of Toronto Schools for seventeen years and won championships in 1927 and 1932.

In 1918 Mr. Rodden was appointed assistant sports editor of the Toronto Globe and from 1928 to 1936 was sports editor. He joined the Kingston Whig Standard as sports editor in 1944 and retired in 1958. He continued to write his weekly column "Sports Highways" for several years after retirement from the Whig Standard. Mike passed away on January 11th 1978 at the age of 87.

INTRODUCTION

In assuming the onerous task of writing a book about my experiences in sport and in other fields of endeavour I have bowed to numerous suggestions made that my knowledge about athletes, teams and sports history would be of national interest. And thus the die has been cast for better or for worse. In the main I write from memory which is still a verdant green.

It has been my good fortune to coach and collaborate with an army of athletes so vast that it would be impossible to do justice to them all. As a competitor I participated in lacrosse, baseball, hockey, football, boxing, bowling, canoeing and in an alleged sport called "hookstag" which was popular in Mattawa, my home town, during the '90s and the early years of this century.

When I began this book-writing task I quickly discovered that continuity demanded that I must include experiences gained in the Ontario northland as a part-time miner, a prospector but, in the main, fire ranging and canoeing in the wild Abitibi River; roaring Nighthawk Lake; and the dreaded Abitibi Lake, which some maintain is the roughest in the world.

During the five summer seasons in years when I was a university student and athlete I was a fire ranger and game warden on the river and lakes mentioned, and many years later I filled the same posts in Algonquin Park and in the Shining Tree district.

Late in 1909 and early in 1910, I was a member of the Timmins assessment gang in the Porcupine gold fields and there I met some very quaint characters.

In July of the 1911 season I helped to fight the great forest fire that destroyed the West Dome Mine where 19 lives were lost, levelled South Porcupine and Pottsville to ashes and left Cochrane in ruins.

Two of my best friends, Marshall Morrison, who had been a brilliant professional hockeyist in Toronto and Haileybury, and Angus Burt, an assayer from Cleveland, Ohio, lost their lives in that inferno. More than 80 others met a similar fate with the heaviest casualties occurring in the West Dome mine shaft.

I went from Matheson to Golden City, on the east shore of Porcupine Lake, aboard the second relief train and, thereof, I later tell harrowing details that have never been publicized before. I was then only 20 years of age but owing to the illness and absence of Fire Chief Fred Gagnon I had suddenly found myself in command of those courageous men who built a bush road just north of Matheson and saved that village and adjoining McDougall's Chutes from destruction.

The second relief train to Porcupine was jammed with brave men rushing to the assistance of the stricken, the homeless and the injured. That trip was made in the darkness of night, the while countless rabbits huddled between or near the tracks and formed a long, eerie path of death.

As the train slowly ploughed ahead and slithered over those doomed creatures to the left and to the right of us we could see others so tightly jammed together that they seemed to form a solid, brownish carpet. Bears and deer swam in the lakes and the winding Porcupine River and the former were so frightened that they wouldn't have attacked a human being.

More details will be presented as the story unfolds.

As a hockey referee I officiated in 2,864 games; a record never approached by any other arbiter and yet it was by accident – and certainly not by choice – that I entered that arduous trade.

Owing to circumstances over which I had had little control I didn't participate in many hockey games before I was a student at Queen's University during the 1910-11 season. I also had drifted away from baseball and lacrosse but I had had ample opportunity to participate in football.

When I was only 17 years of age I organized, coached and played for the University of Ottawa juniors who captured the intra-mural, the Ottawa City and the Ottawa Valley football titles. In recognition of such services rendered I was demoted to playing ranks on the eve of the Ottawa City-Ottawa Valley sudden-death playoff against the Renfrew CI team on the latter's field.

Ironically enough, Ottawa University won that game 20 to 6 and I scored all the Garnet and Grey's points via four touchdowns. During the years that followed I tutored the following championship or runner-up machines.

1912 – Arts, intra-mural Queen's.

1913 – Meds, intra-mural Queen's.

1916 – Kingston CI – Interscholastic Union eastern titleholders.

1919 - '20 and '21 – Toronto De la Salle juniors who captured one Toronto-Hamilton title and were runners-up for the Interscholastic Union crown once.

1918 – Excelsiors – runners-up for ORFU junior title.

1919 – Toronto Capitals, runners-up to Petrolia for ORFU title.

1919 – Toronto YMCA juniors, Interscholastic Union city champions.

1923 – Meds, runners-up for Mulock Cup title.

1922 to 1938 – University of Toronto Schools who won the interscholastic title in 1925 and 1933 and were runners-up three times.

Senior Record

1920 – Argonauts, Interprovincial Union champions, conquerors of TR & AA, ORFU titleholders, and runners-up to University of Toronto for the Grey Cup.

1921 – Parkdale Canoe Club, ORFU champions and runners-up Argonauts for eastern Canada title.

1922 – Parkdale Canoe Club; ORFU champions. (Note - After Parkdale won the ORFU title for the second consecutive season without losing a league game I resigned and less than two weeks later Argonauts crushed the Paddlers 20 to 1 in the eastern Canada semi-final).

1924 – I took over coaching command of the Balmy Beach team late in the season in preparation for the Grey Cup final against Queen's University which the Gaels won 11-3.

1926 – Argonauts, who finished second in the "Big Four" race and who in their farewell appearance crushed Ottawa Rough Riders, Grey Cup holders, 23 to 0.

1927 – Hamilton Tigers who won the "Big Four" crown; beat Queen's in the eastern semi-final in Kingston 21-6 and lost 9-6 to Balmy Beach in the Grey Cup final in Toronto.

1928 – Hamilton Tigers who went undefeated through the "Big Four" campaign; beat the University of Toronto, ORFU champions, by 28 to 5 and blanked the Regina Roughriders in the cup final 30 to 0.

1929 – Hamilton Tigers won "Big Four" title, vanquished Sarnia in Hamilton 14-2; beat Queen's in Kingston 14-3 and coasted to a 14-3 triumph over Regina with the Grey Cup at stake.

1930 – Hamilton Tigers – Established the all-time record by capturing the union title for the fourth consecutive time after they had won seven exhibition games in Western Canada. The Tigers, riddled with injuries, staggered to an 8-3 conquest of the Queen's University Gaels but bowed out 8-5 to Balmy Beach in the eastern final. Only ten points; another all-time record, were scored against those Bengals in the six "Big Four" games.

During the four seasons I tutored the Bengals they won, inclusive of exhibition tests, 39 games, tied two and lost four. It is a record unapproached in Canadian football history and it is likely to withstand the assaults of time. I was also the first mentor ever to guide five teams in Grey Cup finals.

I coached 44 teams during my career and won 27 titles. Yet, the highest salary I ever received did not exceed $1,500 and I reached that "pinnacle" twice – in 1928 and 1929 – when in those two races combined only one defeat was registered against the Hamilton Tigers.

I returned to the Tigers seven years later but very few players of senior calibre were in the squad and the team garnered only two victories both at the expense of the high-rated and forward-passing Montreal Winged Wheelers. At season's end I retired permanently from the senior coaching field.

In September 1918, I launched my sports writing career as assistant-editor with the Toronto Globe. Later I became sports editor, a post I held until 1936.

In 1944 I became Sports Editor of the Kingston Whig-Standard and remained at that post until January 1st, 1959, when I became a columnist for the same fine newspaper.

I sincerely trust that readers of "My Life's History" will not be critical of the use of the word "I". Any success I achieved in sport I attribute to the stars who played under my command and to all others, notably hockeyists, who tolerated my officiating.

No less than eight of the first 15 aces elected to the Football Hall of Fame were my former proteges. Two of them—Harry Batstone and the late Lionel Conacher, played under my direction before they made their senior debuts, and another, Dave Sprague, was promoted to similar status by me.

CHAPTER I

The Story Begins

The story begins in the picturesque little mountain town of Mattawa where I was born in a small house at the foot of the Laurentian Hills on a wild and stormy night on April 24, 1891. I learned very early in life that one must take the bitter with the sweet. My parents, who had been school teachers, were not blessed with wealth but they kept the faith, the while each carried a flaming torch in the right.

I was the second of four children, the oldest of whom was John; the third Mary and the youngest Edmund Anthony. John, who was born in 1889, was so quiet and reserved that he unwittingly invited verbal and physical abuse by rowdies in that tough lumbering town that was composed of English, Irish, Scottish, French, Indian and halfbreed citizens.

My father, Bernard Edward, was an auditor of renown who had been born in Douglas, Ontario in 1847. He was the only child in the family. My mother, Margaret Matilda Dowdall, was born at Wayside, near Perth, in 1862 or during the Civil War in the United States.

My paternal grandparents, who had crossed the sea from Ireland, died before my parents' marriage. They settled in Douglas, Ontario, but allegedly, my grandfather eventually sailed for Australia, seeking gold, and with all others aboard he lost his life when the ship sank in the Pacific Ocean.

My maternal grandparents, whose father and mother were Irish immigrants, had eight children, all of whom have answered the "Last Call", Patrick Sylvester Dowdall, Peter, Mary, Margaret, Edward, John, James and Bernadette. All were in attendance at my grandparents' "Golden Wedding". My mother, who died in her ninetieth year, lived longer than did any of her brothers and sisters but Peter, James and Bernadette survived until they were in the high 80's.

As far back as I can remember – and that, believe it or not, takes in the early 90's, I was keenly interested in sports. So was my father who would have been a great athlete if circumstances hadn't impelled him to become a wage earner when he was in his early 'teens. Factually, at the age of only 19 he was the school principal in Douglas.

We were a close-knit and deeply religious family and my parents preached a gospel of friendship and tolerance to our fellow men. Mattawa, a cosmopolitan town, was a kind of "League of Nations" in that it was inhabited by members of so many nationalities.

The name Mattawa is Indian and its translation is "Meeting of Waters", indicative of the fact that the waters of the Mattawa river flow into the Ottawa in that scenic Laurentian Hills setting. The Mattawa river proper is only three miles long but it is a fast-running stream, beset with danger for the unwary.

Adjacent to the river lies Squaw Valley wherein resided most of the

Indian and halfbreed citizens. Our family lived during many of those years at the top of a hill which to this day is known as "Roddens' Hill" although officially it was never so designated by the town council. The old homestead still stands on, a bit majestic in the sun.

My brother John, who abhorred violence, began his school career in 1894 at the age of five and almost immediately discovered that he would have to fight or flee from his assailants, it being the custom of the time to so operate.

John, called Jack, used discretion and in the interest of peace ignored the valor attached.

When I reached the age of five on April 24th, 1896, I didn't have much time to celebrate because I was hustled off to St. Anne's school the very next day. During the first recess I was assailed by an older boy and I absorbed a bad beating during the process. I did not choose to run and during the next ten years it has been estimated that I participated in at least 32 battles and won nearly all of them.

When we were very young Jack and I built a bobsled which, miraculously enough, was the fastest in the town. The bobsled run began in the Laurentian Hills just north of our home, crossed a long stretch of slightly slanted ice-terrain, went down Roddens' Hill, through Squaw Valley, down another hill and out onto the frozen Mattawa river. To make it swifter we applied water to the hill and hereafter comparatively few challenged us for supremacy.

During those memorable years we lost only one race and on that occasion the running line we were in at the foot of Roddens' Hill, had been deliberately salted. I was the steersman and when we struck terra firma while travelling at blinding speed I was propelled through the air and in a fraction of a second Jack landed on my back.

On occasions in the darkness of evening or in moonlight sleighing parties were staged on that treacherous course. So congested did the hill become that parties returning for another thrilling ride had to use one of two other hills to reach the starting point.

By mutual agreement horse-drawn sleighs were denied the privilege of using Roddens' Hill but one eventful afternoon the late Henri Timmins, delivering parcels from the store, broke that unwritten rule. The horse he guided was noted for his balky attitude and he had figured in one runaway that nearly cost the lives of Henri Timmins and two nuns.

As ill-fortune would have it I, alone on the bobsled, reached the crest of the hill before I saw the horse. To swerve from the course would have been risky and unwise so I lowered my head and body, struck the horse on the two front feet, skimmed beneath the hind ones and went under the sleigh.

On another occasion at the foot of the schoolhouse hill where a fence blotted out the view, our bobsled, with Jack, Michel François and myself aboard, struck the same horse on the hind legs. The impetus carried me into the open spaces beyond but the sleigh impaled François, the while Jack crashed against the vehicle.

Thereafter we avoided such risks by having a boy act as a lookout at the foot of that hill. Henri Timmins also took precautions, probably because his family – who later became fabulously wealthy – couldn't then afford to buy another horse.

Mattawa was unique in that it actually was composed of three villages. All stores and no less than five hotels were located on the south side of the Mattawa river. That section was known as Mattawan. Rosemount and Squaw Valley were situated on the north side and there was one hotel called the Rosemount which in the dark 90's was owned by a man named Peter Lamothe. Later it was bought by a Mr. Gaudette.

Great rivalry prevailed between the North and the South and it was given free rein when hookstag games were waged between factional teams on a field called Rankin's Point. Hookstag sticks were made of maple or hickory. Two small rubber balls attached to a strap formed the scoring missile.

By diligent practice players became experts in catching and throwing that hard-to-handle double sphere. The so-called sport reeked with peril and was much rougher than was lacrosse, a game in which Mattawa teams excelled. Casualties were painfully numerous and following a riotous exhibition in 1905 the town's lone policeman ruled that there must be no more of that.

In that farewell contest the Rosemounts clashed against the Stations from Mattawan and the carnage was terrific. I was the youngest player on the firing line that evening and I absorbed so many head bruises that several weeks elapsed before I could again wear a cap.

The Mattawans were the older and heavier team and in Gordon Shanks they had a stellar goalkeeper. The Rosemounts were the swifter and more elusive operators. We also had fashioned an attack in which the pellet was tossed around with abandon. Probably owing to good fortune or the breaks I collaborated in scoring many goals, the while Shanks, who later moved to the Canadian Soo, was deluged with flying rubber.

Caught in the enveloping storm, the Mattawans began to 'lay on the hickory' and, taking up the challenge and the cudgels, the Rosemounts replied in kind. Down a long trail that I have travelled in football, lacrosse and hockey I have never seen anything that even approached that hookstag duel in regard to downright roughness and brutality.

Reverting to the 90's, I recall many incidents that rate mention. During my first day at school a draw was held with a wax figure of the infant Jesus the prize at stake. When the winning number was announced the holder of the ticket could not be located, the reason being that I couldn't read. However, a girl named Laura Fink found it in my possession just in the nick of time.

With one lone exception it was the only prize I ever drew out of a hat. I did on one occasion win a sprinting race at a school picnic but owing to a false start a re-run was ordered and I finished third. Actually, I had won the first dash without breaking a rule and I so deeply resented the decision rendered that I never participated in another foot race.

In those roaring 90's Mattawa had one of the world's greatest lacrosse teams and owing to the fact that they practiced and staged games at the Fairgrounds, a long stone's throw from our home, I seldom missed a workout. On that playing field, which was situated at the foot of the mountains and was adjacent to two cemeteries, I idolized those gifted athletes and wistfully hoped that eventually I would join them.

The greatest of them all was "Miyah" Quesnell, the slickest stickhandler down memory's lane. He was only a wisp of a fellow but in practice and competition he was wraith-like as he zigged and zagged on scoring sorties. Later I often saw in action all the super-stars of the sport but I never saw an attacker who possessed the wizardry of Quesnell.

There was a year when Mattawa challenged the famous Ottawa Metropolitans for possession of the Minto Cup and it was arranged that a home and home two-games series would be staged with the opener in the Capital. The Mets, scornful of those unknowns from the 'sticks', had expected that one game would be sufficient but they had no way of knowing that the hard-bitten Mattawa team had no peer.

When they realized that they had over-matched themselves the Mets applied the hickory and erred again. In retort cordiale the tough hombres from Mattawa struck back at their assailants and the game deteriorated into a brawl. At its conclusion the Mets led by 2 to 1 and they quite wisely decided that they harbored no ambition to invade the "Meeting of Waters" town.

To say the least, there was seldom a dull day in Mattawa. During river drives the old rickety bridge that spanned the Mattawa river was generally over-crowded with spectators, the while they watched the daring rivermen skillfully breaking up jams by releasing key logs. When all else failed and the screaming logs were piled high into the air experts dislodged them by using dynamite.

In 1905 Booth's Mills logs became so firmly entrenched that even dynamite couldn't set them free. During many hours I watched that battle waged by men against nature and I reached the conclusion that the drivers hadn't detected the key log in the jam. Yet those drivers were experts and the best of them were three men named Fitzgerald, Morrison and Moore.

There was one afternoon when Fitzgerald, a nonswimmer, fell into the swift water under the bridge and would have drowned if I hadn't been there to rescue him. He was lavish in rendering thanks down there beneath the bridge and he asked me, "How old are you?".

I replied that I was 14 and he laughingly said, "I have been rescued by a child." "That could be," I retorted, "but I happen to know where the key log is in that jam." Then I pointed it out and he said "It's worth a try."

Fitzgerald, a brave man in line with his duty, bounded from log to log in the raging rapids and then with one deft twist of the peevy (or peevee) he released that log. Like a roar of thunder the jam broke apart and the hill came tumbling down. Fitzgerald, running for his life, found safety on a large log and flashed under the bridge ahead of the oncoming mountain of timber and water.

Those river drives proper ended after the logs had entered the Ottawa river. Thereafter, sweep gangs released stranded timber, some of them going all the way to the top of the Chaudiere Falls at Ottawa. They were owned by Booth's, and Eddy's of Hull. McLaughlin's of Arnprior and Gilligan's of Mattawa also staged drives annually. Square timbers, brought down in rafts, were shipped overseas from Quebec City.

The running of logs soon became a challenge to me and there was no dare I wouldn't accept. Thereof, when a Mattawan named Charlie

Desarmeau got aboard a huge log and ran the Mattawa river rapids one afternoon I could not resist the temptation to do likewise. Just as Charlie ended his trip he missed his footing and fell into the river but he scrambled to safety.

Although I was wearing a new pair of shoes which were rather slippery, I found a log to my liking the next evening and went bounding through the gorge. I had hoped to avoid a cellar just below the bridge but I failed. The lot hit the chasm and went under but I leaped into the air and alit upon it when it resurfaced.

What I didn't know during that thrilling journey was that my father, one of the country's greatest experts in the logging industry, was watching me from the bridge. Later he did not reprimand me but he must have wondered if I had lost my mind.

There was another logging company called Brunston's and it got its timber from the mountain on the Ontario side of the Ottawa river. However, in 1898 a great forest fire swept over the mountain, leaped the Ottawa to the Laurentian Hills on the Quebec side and destroyed thousands of valuable trees. No more spectacular holocaust ever occurred in the bushlands of the north.

If memory isn't faulty, the fire had its origin high in the mountain about twenty miles west of Mattawa. As it gathered speed, driven by an easterly wind, the swirling smoke appeared to touch the clouds, an ominous warning that the fire would rapidly gain momentum. Experts like my father, Camey MacDonald and Bill Reilly, the Booth's Company foreman, read those signs accurately and knew that much valuable timber was doomed.

At about 7 o'clock that memorable evening the tolling bells atop St. Anne's church alerted Mattawans that the fire was out of control. Even then we could hear the crackling of the falling blaze-plagued trees; many of them red pine that were four feet or wider at the base and had reached majestically into the skies.

Owing to the dense smoke, darkness came early and many of us rushed to the top of the schoolhouse hill where, entranced and alarmed, we watched the fire as it approached the wide Ottawa river. Hope, you know, springs eternal in the human heart, and fervent prayers were said that the wide river would prevent the fire from reaching the Laurentians in Quebec.

Bill Reilly and his crew, however, left nothing to chance and they had crossed the long CPR bridge, there to await and stamp out falling tinders. For several minutes – which seemed to be hours of agonized respite – the holocaust was stymied at the end of the Ontario hills but then, like the roar of Niagara, it burst into a tremendous flame and leaped the river in a matter of seconds. It struck the mountains, which at that point are about 300 feet high, and countless blazes turned night into day. Fires, you know, force air vacuums but do not drown out sound. Thus on that eerie night of long ago we, who stood so far away, could distinctly hear the raucous voice of Bill Reilly as he thundered instructions to his gallant assistants.

We could see the men distinctly as they dashed hither and yon in trying to squelch budding fires at their sources. The fire in the main, was, however, out of control and with the blazing mountains reflected deep in the river there was formed a picture that could never be effaced from the minds of those who saw it.

I do not recall just where the fire ended but it may have been opposite Deux Rivieres. But the church bells tolled no more. The town had escaped destruction and prayers of thankfulness were uttered in homes and in churches. The mountains were knee deep in ashes and the whip-poor-wills who used to sing so lustily in the moonlight had vanished for the nonce.

River drivers are unique in many ways. At least they were in that glamorous long ago. Many of them couldn't swim and those who could toiled in peril in that they wore cumbersome clothes and heavy caulked boots. They were, however, so adept and fearless that they rode those logs with abandon and were not appalled by rapids.

Most of those dare devils cut logs through the winter months and then drove them to the Ottawa. They drew monthly salaries that wavered between $12 and $16, with free board and lodging. The payoff stations were in Mattawa and, loaded with such wealth after having concluded river drives, many of them repaired to hotel bar rooms where celebrations went on for several days.

In Paddy O'Farrell's Ottawa Hotel one of those drivers wagered that he could kick the ceiling with his working shoes. And he accomplished that feat not once, but three times. On another occasion in the same hotel; now the Trans-Canada; a free-for-all broke out which Chief Filion couldn't halt.

Word of the eruption spread quickly through the town and reinforcements were rushed to the scene. A delegated speaker then addressed the rioters and he was so respected – and feared – that order came out of chaos. He didn't waste any words but his message struck no discordant notes.

During one of Booth's drives keen rivalry broke out between two sweep gangs who manned long row boats called 'pointers'. Sixteen men and a steersman formed each crew. The debatable point concerned the matter of speed and by mutual agreement it was decided to stage a three mile race on a Sunday morning.

Having heard about the oncoming duel, twenty-eight youngsters – I wasn't one of them – decided that they would get into the race. They borrowed a pointer, moved to the starting post below McCool's Mill and got into the "swim". Most of them had oars while some used paddles but they held an advantage in that they knew that course like they did the backs of their hands.

It had been estimated that the race would be concluded about 12:30 p.m. and, following services in the various churches, citizens sped to the rickety bridge and jammed the shaky railings. There is a bend in the river about a quarter of a mile from the bridge and it was there that observers first saw the oncoming pointers – but three of them instead of the expected two.

About two minutes later those manning the leading craft could be distinguished and a great roar went up when Jules Timmins, Jimmy Wright, Eddie Gilligan and other youngsters were identified. Straining at the oars the experienced rivermen tried with might and main to overtake those upstarts who had unofficially challenged them for supremacy but pursuit was hopeless and with oars and paddles lifted aloft the kids flashed under the bridge far ahead of the experts.

In another contest of skill, log-birreling and the running from end to end of a so-called log that actually was a long crooked branchless tree, wide at one end and only inches wide at the other, the entrants were Fitzgerald, Morrison and Moore. None succeeded and great laughter ensued when Morrison, who had only one eye, fell into the stream and seemed to be winking at those on the bridge when he surfaced.

Almost immediately debates were aired about the ability or lack of it exposed by that chagrined trio. The consensus was that nobody could run that log from end to end. I thought otherwise and thereof I proceeded to put the matter to a test. I had run thousands of logs and on many occasions I had ignored the bridge and had crossed the river on them.

I discarded my shoes, paddled to the scene on a small raft and ran that log, or tree, from the narrow end to the wide. I was, of course, very light in weight and that made the feat possible. Some of the spectators hurled defiance at me and proclaimed that the log couldn't be run from the opposite direction. I accepted that dare and negotiated the distance, both ways, three times.

CHAPTER 2

In a World of Our Own

Those were thrilling days in a world of our own. There was seldom a dull moment and there was also tragedy and pathos. One evening two French-Canadian girls; Sada and Aida Poirier; went canoeing with two bank clerks but in the fast rapids just above the 'Big White Bridge', which spans the Ottawa river, the craft capsized and one of the Poirier girls was drowned.

A drowning tragedy almost struck our family when my brother Jack got into trouble in the deep water off Rankin's Point. When I saw he was in grave danger I called to two sawyers named John Sauve and Frank Green to rescue him. Sauve, a logging foreman who couldn't swim, rushed into the water up to his shoulders and held Green who grasped Jack just as the latter was going down for the third time.

During that frantic struggle Jack pulled Green below the surface but Green clung to him and Sauve pulled them both to shore. Jack was unconscious for several minutes before he learned that he hadn't gone into the 'Great Beyond'.

Just at that moment a man named Dubois arrived and, having heard about the near-fatality, he advised Jack and myself that, under no circumstances, should we tell our parents about this narrow escape. We promised, but that evening my father informed us that he knew all about the incident.

When I expressed astonishment and offered denials he said, "Why, as I crossed the bridge I met Dubois and he told me all about it". If Dubois had been in the vicinity at that moment I suspect that I would have clouted him with a baseball bat or a hookstag stick.

The following day when I met Mr. Noah Timmins, who several years later purchased the Hollinger Mine for $300,000, he scornfully suggested that I hadn't exhibited courage in failing to go to Jack's rescue. To which I icily replied. "If help had not been so close at hand I would not have hesitated to go to Jack's assistance but I know my limitations as a swimmer and I am aware that I couldn't have rescued Jack and I too would have been drowned."

Later I rescued Jack twice from the Ottawa river and once from the Mattawa. I also saved the life of a boy named Freddy Stover in the Black river near Matheson; prevented five men from going to their deaths over Iroquois Falls and extricated two prospectors who were in grave peril two miles from shore in storm-swept Nighthawk Lake. In addition I in 1915 rescued from imminent death a man named Brogan, a non-swimmer who had fallen out of a canoe and was clinging to a rock below the falls in the onrushing Kowkash river, 320 miles west of Cochrane. Five others rescued could be listed.

I mention the above in justification of my conviction that Mr. Timmins, my father's employer, erred when he questioned my courage.

If I have ever been afraid I was unaware of the fact. This is a difficult story to write because there are all too many who are prone to believe that even the truth has a touch of braggadocia. One's duty, however, supercedes all other considerations.

Mattawa, incidentally, was not a town where boastfulness paid dividends. Its citizens had their trials and tribulations and youngsters learned early in life that they had to fight their own battles. It was a chip-on-the-shoulder town where older boys encouraged younger ones to defend themselves. I tried to keep that faith.

I was assailed, battered and bruised but I fought on, never fearing the consequences. Even to this day those episodes of my childhood are known of and talked about when oldtimers gather in Ike Tongue's Mattawa general store which was formerly owned by the Timmins brothers. When I was admitted to the Hockey Hall of Fame and and was given a CRU football plaque they remembered.

Of all the battles I ever participated in the one that gave me the greatest thrills was that which I waged against a talkative and brash newcomer to the town named Sammy Riopelle. Sammy came in with one of those chips on his shoulder and in rather fast time he lowered a boom on some of the town's most dynamic fisticuffers. Then one night, when of all places, I was returning home from church services, he intercepted me and announced that I was next on the list. That melee was waged in semi-darkness adjacent to Riopelle's home and he emerged from it beaten, broken and cowed. Tough Sammy demanded no encore.

With battles looming to the left of us, the right of us, behind us and in front of us, all had to be very wary. A state of undeclared warfare prevailed between the Mattawans and the Rosemounts and competition was a bit keen between the separate and public schools. There were occasions, too, when the Rosemounts and the Squaw Valley Indians smoked no pipes of peace.

The rink, owned by the Timmins Brothers, was situated in

Mattawan, a mile from our home. It was there that I made my debut as a midget hockeyist, having been selected to guard the goal poles. No nets were used and with leg pads unavailable I inserted magazines in my stockings as protection against flying rubber.

I was aligned with the Rosemounts who won the opener of a three game series 2 to 1. The Rosemount manager, however, decided that I was too young and I was replaced for the second test, which the Mattawans won by 8 to 1. I was then restored to good standing but I declined the invitation to return. The Mattawans won the final game and title with the greatest of ease.

Reverting, I recall that in 1897 I assiduously read the Utica Globe wherein the oncoming heavyweight boxing championship bout between the defender, Jim Corbett, and the challenger, Bob Fitzsimmons, was allotted top prominence. My brother, Jack, was a staunch Corbett supporter and I was in Fitzsimmons' corner.

When the news was flashed that "Fitz" had struck down Corbett by using the previously unheard of solar plexus blow in the fourteenth round Jack maintained that he had won on a foul. I took the negative and it was finally agreed that we would stage a replica of the bout in the backyard.

Jack, who must have studied the Corbett system, won every one minute round that preceded the fourteenth. This called for a bit of fast thinking so I suggested that in the fourteenth he should permit me to hit him in the solar plexus, just to make it an official replica of the original bout.

Jack, with rare good nature, agreed that I had 'hit' no discordant note and went along with the plan. When I connected he went down and rolled around in what we imagined was faked pain. He wasn't, however, playing a part and only copious water applications erased his suffering.

Great excitement prevailed in the "Meeting of Rivers" town during the Spanish-American War; the Boer War and the Russo-Japanese War.

Songs like *"Just Break the News to Mother"*, *"Blue Bell"* and *"We'll Never Let The Old Flag Fall"* became very popular and temporarily replaced *"After The Ball Was Over"*, *"Clementine"* and *"My Old Kentucky Home"*.

During the Spanish-American War, which was launched after the USA battleship Maine was blown up in Havana harbor, Mattawa sportsmen, seeking diversion, brought in the North Bay senior hockey team to play against the home forces. It was also agreed that a return engagement would be staged.

The Bayites, confident of victory, held Mattawa in deep scorn but unknown to them the Timmins brothers and associates had imported three Pembroke aces named Beamish, McVean and Black. Louis Berlinquette, who later played for the Montreal Canadiens, and Adelard Freve were Mattawa's stars.

For 10 cents I gained admission to the small rink wherein there were no seats. Being unable to see the goings-on I climbed high on a rafter and from the dizzy perch I watched the 10-2 slaughtering of the visitors by a team that even in this era would be formidable.

When the disaster was over the battered Bayites climbed into open horse-drawn sleighs and immediately were made the targets of thrown chunks of ice. Quickly they sought refuge under coonskin covers and as the sleighs were pulled swiftly away the assailed players lustily sang *'Blue Bell'* and *"Just Break the News to Mother"*. Owing to the fact that the Mattawa management could see no profit in importing those Pembroke aces for a game in North Bay and, having learned a trick or two from Ottawa Metropolitan lacrosse officials, the Mattawans laughingly forfeited the second test, the while they pointed out that the Bayites couldn't beat Mattawa's combined school team by a margin of eight goals.

Feuds between localities have not been uncommon and in that away-back-when they were dynamically portrayed by Ottawa versus Montreal; Toronto versus Hamilton; Pembroke versus Renfrew; the American and Canadian Soos and by North Bay and Mattawa; to mention a few.

The Mattawa versus North Bay entanglements concerned dominance in lacrosse, football and politics. In the last named field Mattawa consistently provided Liberal and Conservative candidates for the East Nipissing riding. John Loughrin, a hardware merchant, and Dr. Michael James, my godfather, were Liberals, the while Charlie Lamarche, owner of the Mattawa hotel and Harry Morel were the Conservatives' strong men.

Both parties were in mutual agreement only in that each insisted that the Georgian Bay canal route, stretching from Georgian Bay to Ottawa, would pass through the French river, into Lake Nipissing and thence through three lakes – Trout, Talon and Champlain – along the Mattawa river and into the Ottawa. No greater political football was ever kicked around.

The bridge that spanned the Mattawa river was also given the full treatment. It was such a broken-down wood monstrosity that when a circus came to Mattawa elephants were taken from Mattawan to Rosemount through the rock-strewn Mattawa river. A new bridge was mandatory and in election time each party vied with the other in promising that a modern bridge would be erected.

Dr. James, whose office was across the main street from the Timmins store, vociferously proclaimed during one heated pre-election campaign that the bridge and canal would become realities. Voters were also assured by representatives of the warring parties that Mattawa would be made the county seat and that a railroad to the far north would be erected on the Ontario side of the Ottawa river.

Such lavish avowals lured unwary voters into traps and they did live in hope that Mattawa would become the "Gateway to the North". The only promise ever honored was the erection of a new stone bridge which still stands. On the eve of one election early in this century the Conservatives placed the following sign high in the air at the Mattawan side of the old bridge – "Vote for Dr. James and and the Old Hoss Will Eat Grass".

James, a Queen's University graduate and a brilliant doctor, was defeated in another election by Morel and the latter hastened to Toronto where he tried to convince Premier J.P. Whitney that all promises made to the Mattawa electorate would be kept. Whitney, however, had more important matters to attend to and Morel was given the run-around.

In that emergency, Morel retired to the Parliament Buildings hall and there he sat resolutely on a chair. When approached he firmly stated that he would remain in that position until Whitney surrendered. Whitney did and Mattawa became the beneficiary.

Lamarche, who originally broke Liberal dominance in East Nipissing, was not an educated man and when in lieu of another promise made that the East Nipissing member elect would be made the Minister of Lands, Forests and Mines, he demanded action his plea was rejected. Thereof, it was proposed that Lamarche would accept a judgeship at $5,000 a year and that Frank Cochrane, a hardware merchant from the tiny village of Rutherglen would be taken into the cabinet.

Torn between conflicting emotions, Lamarche sought advice from my father who had been assured that he would be the next Minister of Lands, Forests and Mines. My father advised him to abide by his promises and probably pointed out that East Nipissing electors would never send Cochrane to Parliament.

Lamarche, however, resigned and Cochrane, who held the Lands, Forests and Mines portfolio for years eventually became the Minister of Railroads and Canals in the Dominion Government although he never participated in an election. His is a record beyond compare.

Following Lamarche's resignation a party in honor of Cochrane was held in the Mattawa Harmony Hall – but harmony was more imaginary than real. After the 'Ball was Over' Cochrane – after whom the town of Cochrane is named – slipped as he was about to get aboard the CPR Imperial Limited and one of his legs was severed by the wheels.

Frank Cochrane was a very fine and dedicated man and I, among many, owe him a debt of gratitude. During the summer seasons of 1910, '11, '12 '13 and '14, I was, mainly through his influence, employed as a fire ranger and game warden under the jurisdiction of the Ontario Government. And those were never-to-be-forgotten years.

The Timmins brothers, who married sisters named Pare, became interested in mining pursuits during or before the '90s. Hundreds of ore samples lay on shelves in my father's office in the Timmins store. My father, incidentally, became one of two owners of a nickel property 32 miles west of Sudbury in 1882. It was never developed and those 252 acres, five miles away from the Worthington property, are still owned by my brothers, my sisters and myself.

Stories about gold in the north were rampant in Mattawa after an Indian named Jocko allegedly returned from that country with gold in his packsack. Many years, however, elapsed before that dream came true and when it did Noah Timmins, acting independently of his silver mining partners, Henry Timmins, D.A. Dunlop, also of Mattawa, and John and Duncan McMartin of Cornwall, purchased the Hollinger Mine for $300,000 and when his former associates returned all went on from there to acquire other properties and fabulous wealth.

The Timmins brothers, Henry and Noah, were drastically apart in stature and in ideology but both followed the same star in mining pursuits. They were, however, a bit fortunate when they struck riches in silver-laden Cobalt terrain. Factually, they were providing supplies for the McMartin railroad construction company when a blacksmith named Fred LaRose discovered a silver sidewalk and reported his find to Noah Timmins. The latter knew silver when he saw it and in fast time the property was purchased for $25,000 and the original company was formed. Reference to this will be made later on in the story.

CHAPTER 3

Vivid Are Those Memories

Among characters in Mattawa I vividly remember were an English lord named Earl; a Parisian named Ribout, who had survived the Franco-Prussian War in 1870; Barclay Gilligan, owner of a saw mill; Joe Tenesco, one of the most gifted athletes I have ever known; Arthur Ferland, who married Timmins' sister; Severe Payette, an hotel owner; Dr. C. W. Haentchel, a brilliant lacrosse player, and Sam Tongue, who would have been an ace in Bisley rifle marksmanship.

Ferland, who had nine children, almost became the owner of all the best mines in the Cobalt district. In the final summation, however, he had to settle for part ownership of the O'Brien-Ferland Mine, which adjoined the LaRose. Later he sold his interests to O'Brien and formed the Ferland-Chalmers Company.

Tenesco, an Indian, was unique in that he kept aloof from trouble unless provoked. Although options were limited this 230 pound giant became proficient in baseball, lacrosse and canoeing. Light of foot, he once turned a birch bark canoe upside down, stood upon it and ran the rapids under the Mattawa bridge.

I have coached many famous football players during my career but I have no hesitation in saying that Tenesco would have become one of the super-stars of the gridiron. A man of terrific speed afoot, he once was matched against a trotter at the Fairgrounds; the stipulation being that he would be given a one eighth mile handicap advance in a half mile race. He won with plenty to spare.

Lord Earl, who owned a small candy store on the Main Street, was a little man who didn't appear to have any friends. Daily he hopefully sat on the verandah awaiting customers who never came. In the windows candy melted in the sun and popcorn bags became covered with dust. His store, standing well back from the street, was given a wide berth.

One sultry summer afternoon, as I watched him in wonder, and sympathy, I decided that I would cross the Rubicon and purchase some popcorn. Always the rebel, I didn't particularly care whether or not my action would be approved. The old man smiled when I approached him and he politely asked "What can I do for you?".

I answered "I have a few pennies and I would like to buy some popcorn." "Right this way", he replied "and you can have the best in the house. I always aim to please and thank you very much." I bought three bags of that mildewed popcorn and then, later, I tossed them into the river.

When Lord Earl died there were few mourners. He was buried in the Protestant cemetery, there to rest eternally. Two years later my brother Jack and I visited that burial place and there we saw that Lord Earl's grave had fallen apart in the spring thaw. Deep holes or ruts reached almost to the coffin and in the grass there lay a tin cross.

When I attempted to adjust the cross a snake scrambled out and fled into the weeds. Momentarily, Jack and I became a bit superstitious but we rallied quickly and then we did make the grave presentable. Together we knelt and we prayed that in that other land Lord Earl would know no grief. Fate had not been kind to him but we felt that at long last he had gone 'home'.

As we turned away I repeated the immortal words of the poet Gray; "the boast of heraldry' the pomp of power or all that beauty or that life e're gave await, alike, that inevitable hour, 'The paths of glory lead but to the grave."

Mr. Ribout, who lived on the fringe of Squaw Valley, had four children. The mother of two of them; a daughter and a son; had died in Paris and he had later married a gifted lady of the nobility whose parents had been ruined financially as a result of the Franco-Prussian War. Two sons, Fernand and Gaston, were born of that marriage.

The daughter married a shoemaker named Guimond whose hobby was honey-producing bees. Early in the century the Guimonds moved into a house next to ours but with a wide field intervening. It was in that field that Jack and I raised enough vegetables to supply our family the year around but those buzzing bees were a problem.

During the raspberry season in 1904 my mother briefly left a large pot boiling on the stove in the summer kitchen and when she returned she found that hundreds of bees had perished in that steaming heat. They lay more than an inch in depth, the while others buzzed around the kitchen in droves.

Having surveyed the scene, my mother sent me post haste in pursuit of Guimond and, with equal speed, he returned with a fan in each hand and large bits of cloth covering his arms, head and most of his face. What he said, I did not understand because he spoke in French but the surviving bees caught the message and they fled from that kitchen and back to their hives.

Mrs. Ribout, a talented musician, singer, organ and piano player, was the organist in St. Anne's church and most of the time I pumped air into the organ. The choir, as a whole, was one of the finest ever assembled and Mrs. Ribout was a star in the cast.

I do not recall the year but on a summer evening just before darkness rolled out of the hills, Mr. Ribout came dashing along the street that fronted our home. When he espied me he asked in a trembling voice "Have you seen Mrs. Ribout? She has vanished and I am terribly worried."

Mrs. Ribout had had a nervous breakdown and Annie Clement, our former maid, had been employed to be her protective companion. Annie, however, had other duties that demanded attention and that afternoon while she was absent for a few minutes Mrs. Ribout wandered away.

When I assured Mr. Ribout that his wife had not passed our home he turned back. Assistance was solicited and a searcher found Mrs. Ribout's body floating in the Ottawa river near Gilligan's Rock where the water is fast and deep. Her cape had kept her body on the surface.

An entire town mourned the tragic passing of this gifted lady whose graciousness of manner and whose musical talent had endeared her to all. As I watched her as she lay in her flower-covered coffin I was entranced by her hands which were exceedingly small. In them she held her beads and crucifix and although I was just a child I was broken-hearted.

Fernand Ribout, who was one of my best friends, would not be consoled. He was born aboard ship while en route to Canada and he probably never knew if he was a French national or a native of this country. He was, however, consumed with hatred of Kaiser Wilhelm and of Germany and when war came in 1914 he enlisted and later distinguished himself on the battlefields of Europe.

Today he, his brothers and his sister lie in a Mattawa cemetery but the old brick home in the valley still stands as do many others that were built so long ago. The forest that adjoined that house and surrounded Squaw Valley has, however, vanished, leaving desolation but memories live on.

In the Ottawa river near Rankin's Point there is an eddy where logs and floating debris often became trapped. There after the sun went down fish called mooneyes leaped out of the water in thousands, forming a picturesque phenomenon. These were eatable when the water was cold but, otherwise, they were no delicacy.

That eddy fascinated us but only the daring swam in the vicinity. Quick sand stretched far out from Rankin's Point and those who sold fresh water gave that shore a wide berth. Occasionally, however, drivers of horses would back wagons and barrels about thirty feet in the stream.

It was a risky business and one afternoon the quicksand claimed a heavy toll when John Loughrin's hired man and a team of horses lost their lives in the whirlpool. The wagon also sank and was beyond recovery.

A neighbour, wife of the chief fire ranger, had a cat which had become a nightly nuisance with its eerie wailing. It was a beautiful animal but in the interests of complaining neighbors it was decided that the meow expert must be dispatched into Valhalla. Daily, at five cents per pail, I used to carry spring water a long way from John Laughrin's well to this neighbor's household so it wasn't any wonder that in desperation, she asked me to dispose of the cat.

It was an assignment that did not appeal to me but I did try to eliminate the cat by hitting him with numerous rocks. That treatment did him no good but the cat, who had been my friend, looked askance at me thereafter. Try as I could I was unable to catch him but finally on a torrid day he lay down at the foot of a large pine tree and I nabbed him when he was asleep.

Having deposited his catship in a potato bag I applied a stout string to the top of the bag and, via a rowboat, I took him to the middle of that Ottawa river whirlpool. I felt a bit guilty before and after that cat and bag vanished into the depths but I took solace in the thought that there was no other way.

The next morning I notified the neighbor that my mission had been completed but she retorted a bit icily "If you look behind that stove you will discover that the cat came back. He was wringing wet when he came scratching at the door and unless he succumbs to a cold he will still be a member of the family."

That cat had earned a reprieve and he had provided ample evidence that he had 'nine lives'. As the years rolled on he became less vociferous and his popularity grew apace. But never at any time did he extend a paw of friendship to me, the while he did sombrely gaze at me in exhibiting suspicion.

Among the most laughable incidents I ever remember occurred one inky-black night on the Mattawa bridge. Peter Lamothe, the bad tempered owner of the Rosemount hotel, had incurred the wrath of some of Mattawan's leading citizens and eventually the latter decided to teach him a lesson.

Lamothe had a horse-driven bus that was in charge of a Negro employee and every morning and night of each day that bus was taken the mile journey across the Mattawa bridge and to the CPR station, there to be at the service of hotel customers. Thereof, the plotters decided that it would be a splendid idea to place wire fences on the bridge and thus make train connections impossible. The said schemers were, however, faced with one problem that demanded consideration. They had no quarrel with the Negro handyman so they made it their business to warn him that he must not cross the bridge that night. He took the hint and when, at the last moment, he refused to make the journey Lamothe defiantly grasped the reins and was on his way.

About midway on the bridge the horses suddenly became balky and no amount of urging could make them proceed. Lamothe, who had anticipated some such effrontery, grasped a pair of pliers and cut down the wire barrier. There were no lights and in the inky darkness he could only see a few feet ahead of him.

The nervous horses went another fifty feet or so before they crashed into the next barrier. Lamothe removed that one but when he reached a third impasse he heard the train moving out of the station. In great indignation, he reversed the procedure and started homeward. But a bridge had been swiftly erected behind him and his spirited horses could stand no more.

Breaking wildly from restraint, they leaped over the railing, crashed into the river and were drowned. It was a lamentable exposition of wit or vengeance but it convinced Lamothe that he had outlived his welcome in the "Meeting of Waters" town.

Lamothe had a brother named George who owned the only bakery in the town. This store, on Main Street, was shaped like a loaf of bread. It was small and made of brick. Lamothe, an Aesop in story-telling, participated in many mayoralty races but was never elected during the years that preceded the exodus of many prominent citizens to the mine-laden north.

Thereafter he held the post, generally by acclamation, for 36 consecutive years. In addition he was a magistrate beyond compare. Allegedly, on occasions, he rendered verdicts that would have put King Solomon to shame. Following a fistic battle waged in Boom Creek on the western outskirts of the town the winner, an Indian named Alexandre, was hailed to court under the jury system. The charge was a serious one and Alexandre employed a North Bay lawyer named Bull to defend him.

Witnesses were in such violent disagreement, some blaming one and some the other, that the jury acquitted Alexandre. Thereof, arguments, mingled with cheers and boos, broke out in the courthouse. Lamothe, having stilled the outcries, then rendered the following verdict, coupled with an oration.

"Gentlemen of the jury, you have found the guilty innocent. Your incompetence confers a black mark on Canadian jurisprudence. Alexandre, you have been acquitted by your so-called peers but you are a disgrace not only to Boom Creek, Mattawa, the district of Nipissing and Ontario but you are also a disgrace to Canada and to the British Empire. I must not and I cannot condone your reprehensible conduct. You must pay the penalty for your crime. Thereof, I sentence you to six months in jail and may the Lord have mercy upon you."

Lawyer Bull, astounded, arose in haste and thundered. "But you cannot sentence this man. He has been found innocent of this charge by his peers. I must demand that justice should be served. Your verdict is not in accordance with the laws of Canada, let alone the British Empire."

Gazing sternly at the lawyer, Lamothe orated as follows. "I have spoken. My decision may not be in accordance with law existent in Ontario, Canada or the British Isles but this is the law of Mattawa and the verdict stands." And it did.

In another case – Lamothe was not the judge – a man named Simpson was accused of theft, the sum being considerable, so he hired a brilliant Tom McGarry, my cousin who resided in Renfrew, and the goings-on became a bit hectic. Under cross-examination McGarry made all witnesses regret that they had been summonsed to court. Acquittal followed and Simpson, a bit grateful, invited McGarry to be his guest in the near-by Ottawa hotel bar room. (That hotel is now the Trans Canada).

McGarry, who was coming to dinner at our home that evening, icily eyed Simpson, who was a plasterer and paperhanger, and acidly remarked. "I wouldn't be seen at a dog fight with you. You are as guilty as can be and I want neither truck nor trade with you."

McGarry, who never lost a murder trial, later defended an Italian sectionman who had been charged with slaying a companion east of Mattawa. The evidence was quite clear, the while young Charlie

McManus, son of the section foreman, told how he discovered the victim covered with brush in the forest.

Undaunted, McGarry so belabored the witnesses with rapid fire comment that they became utterly confused. As the case progressed the conviction became pronounced that if there was any one man in the country who would not commit a murder he was the accused.

The non-plussed jurymen brought in a verdict of innocence and the Italian extended his hand to McGarry in rendering thanks. McGarry's reaction was drastic and fantastic. Said he, "You can thank your lucky stars that you have been acquitted. Your guilt is undeniable. If in future you get into trouble don't send for me."

McGarry, cool as Arctic ice, joined us that evening at dinner and it was then, I imagine, that I looked into the future and imagined that I would eventually be a lawyer. It was a dream unfulfilled and I still have my regrets. That Italian who escaped punishment in Mattawa later murdered a man in Sault Ste. Marie and, I believe, he was the first man ever hanged in the locality.

When he was arrested he sent for McGarry but the latter wasn't interested and, anyway, he had warned him that never again would he defend a man who was so palpably guilty.

McGarry, one of the youngest men ever to graduate from Osgood Hall, set up a law office in Renfrew where his brother Ned was later a hardware merchant. He was just 20 years of age and his pretensions were not taken seriously. My maternal grandmother was one of his first clients and he won that case. However, his advertising shingle didn't tinkle like the bells on a Santa Claus' sled.

Presumably, there were occasions when McGarry regretted that he hadn't remained 'down on the farm'. But he got a 'break' eventually and when that opportunity knocked he did not fail. A man, who was penniless and had a large family, stole a pig but owing to distressing circumstances he was permitted to enjoy freedom before the trial began.

During that interim he approached McGarry who immediately asked him if he had stolen the pig. The reply being in the affirmative, McGarry advised him that nothing could be done in his behalf. With a heavy heart, the culprit turned away but suddenly McGarry stopped him and inquired;

"Have you still got that entire pig?" On being assured that such was the 'case' McGarry directed him to cut the pig exactly in half right down to the last ounce and that he then must bring one half to McGarry's office. When this deed was accomplished McGarry said; "I will be in court tomorrow morning when you go on trial and although I will not defend you I will act as a witness."

In great astonishment, no doubt, the unhappy man departed but in court the next day he asked the magistrate to call McGarry as a witness. The judge, who knew McGarry well – but apparently not well enough – collaborated and when he asked McGarry what he knew about the case the resourceful Thomas replied; "I am willing to take an oath that this man has no more of that pig than I have."

"Well, in that event", said his lordship," the case is dismissed."

McGarry had a dog which he prized highly but, as was the custom in those days, the canine was permitted to run at large. Naturally, he foraged for food and while so doing he pilfered a steak from a butcher shop. He was caught in the act and one of the store owners, who was noted for his wit, asked McGarry what should be done under the circumstances.

McGarry, who had no idea that his own dog had been the raider, replied; "Send a bill to the owner". The butcher then handed him a bill claiming five dollars for loss of the meat and alleged suffering. McGarry glanced at it; paid the damages and strode out.

Two days later when the owner opened his mail he found a bill from McGarry demanding $10.00 for legal advice.

Many such tales could be told about McGarry, who later became the Attorney-General in the Ontario Conservative cabinet. He died in Toronto a long time ago but memories of him are still as verdant green as are Irish shamrocks.

John Loughrin, MPP, was related to McGarry but he was a staunch Liberal. His hardware store stood directly across the street from a dry goods store owned by big Bill Hogarth, a dynamic Conservative. They were both heavy-set men and when they had nothing else to do they traded uncensored insults that startled all listeners.

Hogarth's son Donald, an outstanding lacrosse player, found riches in the mining fields and became one of Canada's wealthiest men. Unofficially, it has been estimated that he reached the $200,000,000 bracket. He was life insured for at least a cool $5,000,000.

Mr. Loughrin had a great sense of humor and he was also a kindly man. My father used to audit his books and in one election he voted for Mr. Loughrin. When another election rolled around my father voted for Charlie Lamarche, the Conservative standard-bearer, and he so notified Mr. Loughrin.

Lamarche was elected and when my father said "Good morning' to Mr. Loughrin the next day, the latter made no reply. Thereof, my father averred that if they ever spoke again Mr. Loughrin would have to make the first overture.

Several years later Mr. Loughrin visited the LaRose Mine in Cobalt where my father was the bookkeeper and auditor. "Good day, Barney", said Mr. Loughrin and my father answered "Good day, John." And thus two Irishmen bridged a gap that should never have been created.

Mr. Loughrin's wit is exemplified in the following factual story. On a hot summer [day] he attached a long black thread to a $10 bill which he placed on the wooden sidewalk near his store. As each passerby espied the prize he or she stooped to retrieve it but Loughrin slyly kept pulling it away in spurts until it was again in his possession.

Finally, Mr. Loughrin espied the parish priest strolling in his direction and his joy knew no bounds. This would be climactic and it was. Instead of stooping to conquer the reverend father stepped upon the green paper, raised it from the sidewalk and deposited it in his purse. Mr. Loughrin had more than met his match.

Mr. John Mooney, a relative of Mr. Loughrin, was a native of Ireland who operated a fruit store on Main Street. Naturally, he dealt in bananas and there came a day when a tarantula awoke in time to find that it was in a northern town. Its appearance engendered excitement and fear but it was quickly executed.

Mr. Mooney, branching out, as it were, became the first merchant to import grapefruit to the town. Under the impression that these were large pale oranges I bought one for five cents and hastened home to enjoy the feast. But when I took that first nibble and found that the fruit was so bitterly sour I tossed it at a squirrel in a tree and knocked him hors-de-combat.

On another occasion I purchased a box of orange-flakes in Lamothe's bakery store and my indignation soared to tall heights when I discovered that there was no orange taste to the flakes.

CHAPTER 4

Schooldays, Fires & Fishing

School days through nine years and part of another were
kaleidoscopic. A large and pretentious Separate School house erected
in 1894 stood on a hill top just north of the rectory. St. Anne's Church,
next in line, was a costly edifice and was among the finest in the
province. The hospital adjoined it.

All, with the exception of the priests' house, were later destroyed by
fire. The church, with its tall spires and cross shining in the sun, was
the town's most inspirational attraction. After intervening forests had
been felled that glittering cross could be seen from many miles away
by those who approached Mattawa from the west. A number of years
ago the church was struck by lightning during a stormy night and it
was razed to the ground.

The original hospital was demolished by fire early in the century. The Mattawa fire brigade, composed of volunteers, had no chance whatever to extinguish that eruption. The horse-drawn engine in use lacked the power to send streams of water high into the air. Propulsive steam engendered by a wooden fire had its limitations.

When that fire died down of its own volition only a pile of smoldering timber, ashes and iron beds remained. Brave men, who had brought all patients to safety, had attempted to retrieve furniture, beds and valuables but they had failed dismally. With other boys I brought out a few dishes before we were ordered away.

The schoolhouse was the largest in the north. There was a cellar and an adjoining playroom. The rooms proper were situated on two floors and above the second one there was a huge theatre where shows were staged. It was also in that theatre that I saw movies of the heavyweight championship bout in which Jim Jeffries, the "Boilermaker", knocked out Bob Fitzsimmons in the eighth round in 1902.

Two long winding stairs provided access to the theatre and if fire had assailed that structure during a show most of the town's prominent citizens would, undoubtedly, have perished. My mother, an excellent elocutionist, had tutored Jack and me in the art and on several occasions we were included in the casts. Predictions were made that we would go on to achieve fame as actors but that outlook was merely an idle, passing fancy.

Jack, I and my sister Mary entered school in that order a year apart but we all became aligned in the entrance class in the academical season of 1903-04. Grey nuns taught in all classes with the exception of the fourth and fifth where a male principal held the reins.

More concerned with sports than with pursuit of knowledge, I was a problem child in that setting and it wasn't until 1906 that I wrote entrance examinations. Two years previously Jack, Mary, who was then just 11 years of age, Harry Nadon and Eva Payette had been the only official survivors in the most difficult entrance examination paper ever inflicted on this Province.

The list of failure throughout the Province was so appalling that the government launched an investigation and discovered that answers to questions asked had never been taught to pupils. Jack and Mary, unquestionably, had bridged that gap because they had been given added tuition by my mother and father.

Harry Nadon, who was killed in the battle of Givinchy during the First Great War, was one of the most brilliant students I have ever known... Mary, serious and bright, was the darling of the school and she went on from there to establish academic records at the University of Toronto.

Nervousness, brought on by over-indulgence in swimming, deterred me from trying the entrance examination until 1906 and then, to the lasting amazement of all concerned, I finished first in the entire district of East Nipissing. It was a feat that I was not destined to duplicate!

Mr. Gallagher, one of the principals, was quite a character who had a penchant for 'laying on the strap'. I was well acquainted with the pains and aches that cat-o-nine-tails provided. Stoically, I accepted such punishment but one day I reached the limit of my patience, if any, when Mr. Gallagher, for no known reason, called little Mary to the front of the class and ordered her to extend her right hand. He then struck her with the strap. He performed the same operation when he hit her on the left hand. Then he thundered, the while streams of tears ran down her cheeks, "Put out your right hand again."

When he struck Mary the first blow I gripped the desk. When he hit her again I shook like an aspen leaf but when he demanded another "pound of flesh" I leaped from my seat, dashed to Mary's rescue and struck the principal flush upon the chin. In a flash the students in that room became a 'madding throng' and chaos prevailed.

That evening I reported the matter to my father and he departed in haste to confer with Mr. Gallagher. I do not know what he said but it must have been convincing because thereafter Mr. Gallagher never raised a hand or a strap to any girl in the class room.

On still another occasion I took a red squirrel to school via the simple expedient of keeping him hidden in a pocket. About ten minutes later I released him and he promptly scampered up onto pretty Helen Meindel's shoulder. Helen, just as promptly, emitted cries of fright and the squirrel sped away and out through an open window.

Mr. Jones, the new principal, being a bit suspicious, ordered me to sit on a chair in front of the class and during the next two weeks I emulated Jack-in-the-corner. Tiring of occupying such an unenviable place in the 'sun', I eventually rebelled and demanded that I be restored to good 'standing', or was it 'sitting'?! Mr. Jones collaborated and I went on from there to pass the entrance examinations with a record-breaking total in marks.

Previous to 1904 no electric lighting was available for our home and under mother's supervision we studied by lamplight. Those were coal oil lamps and they had to be handled with care. But accidents do occur and in one of these only my mother's indomitable courage and resourcefulness prevented our home from being destroyed by fire.

In February of 1903 my brother, Edmund, who was approaching his second birthday, upset a lamp in his bedroom and it exploded with devastating effect. In a blinding flash the room was ablaze but my mother rushed in among the flames and miraculously rescued Edmund from death.

Mother then called on Jack and me to carry pails of water from the winter kitchen, through the dining room, and hall, up a long flight of steps and along another hall to the fire. Acting in relays, we negotiated that route, going both ways, frantic until mother finally extinguished the blaze.

Eddie was so seriously burned that the bones above his left elbow were plainly visible and the hair on his head had been replaced by two tremendous blisters. His moans were pathetic but in a matter of minutes he sighed and fell soundly asleep.

It was a stormy night and in the bitter cold the snow fled before the gales and drifts piled high on the roads but necessity demanded that medical care must be secured in a hurry. I was elected to make that journey of three quarters of a mile and, fortunately, on arrival Dr. C.W. Haentchel was available for duty.

Dr. Haentchel, as I have previously stated, was a swift man on a lacrosse field and he sprinted all the way to our home, the while I was left far behind. Eddie was still unconscious when I returned and mother was suffering excruciating agony, both mentally and physically.

Dr. Haentchel did everything he could to alleviate the pain endured by my mother and Eddie but it was thought doubtful that the latter would survive. Word was dispatched to my father who was auditing books at Kippawa, thirty-eight miles north of Mattawa, and he caught the first south-bound train.

While en route he told the conductor about Eddie's plight and the trainman said. " Just lately we received a new ointment called Mecca and I recommend it highly." He then gave my father the largest jar of salve I have ever seen. Just as if it were yesterday I can see my father as he came over the brow of the school hill and thence through the deep snow to our home in long, swift strides.

On arrival he quickly applied the salve to Eddie's head, face and arms and to mother's arms and hands. I doubt that Dr. Haentchel approved of such treatment but he raised no objections. My cousin, Katie Kitchen, acted as a volunteer nurse and became, in my opinion, another resourceful Florence Nightingale.

Probably at least ten tortuous days and nights passed before it became apparent that Eddie would survive. He did, however, make a remarkable recovery as witness the fact that he later became a quarterback in the ORFU senior series and played in the National

Hockey League with the Chicago Black Hawks, the Toronto Maple Leafs, the Boston Bruins and the New York Rangers.

At this point I will take time out to state that athletes should not be rushed into stern competition when they are too young and immature. Eddie's career serves as an example. At the age of 12 he was a stickhandling wizard with the Haileybury Rexal juniors. One year later he was aligned with the New Liskeard seniors as a goalkeeper.

In 1914 and 1915 he played centre for the potent Haileybury juniors who never lost a game. In 1917 he joined the Toronto De la Salle juniors who won the OHA title. Thereafter he played for the following championship winning machines - A.R. Clarke, Toronto Industrial League; Dominion Bank of the Toronto Bank League; Toronto Granites, 1923 Allan Cup winners; Windsor Bulldogs, International League champions in 1928-29 and the Boston Bruins, who captured the Stanley Cub that same season. In addition he was the top scorer with London Tecumsehs, International League titleholders.

As a hockeyist I did not achieve that kind of distinction but I was aligned with the Queen's University seniors who won the 1913-14 Intercollegiate Union crown, the last time the Gaels ever performed that feat. I was captain of the Haileybury 1914-15 seniors, who finished the Temiskaming League race as runners-up to the powerful Cobalt Lake Miners. In 1917-18 I was a defenceman with the Toronto St. Patrick's OHA seniors before a serious injury drove me into retirement.

I was coach of the St. Patrick's 1918-19 seniors who eliminated, in group play, the Allan Cup holding Kitchener Greenshirts. In the home and home final series against the mighty Hamilton Tigers I was temporarily relieved of coaching duties and was assigned to defence duty in the opening game which was waged in Hamilton.

The management rendered this remarkable decision owing to the fact that Frank Heffernan, the best defenceman in the OHA series, had been stricken with illness. With Hamilton leading by 3 to 0 at the first intermission I voluntarily retired and assigned Dinny Breen of Haileybury to act as my replacement.

St. Pats rallied strongly but late in the action the racing Tigers scored six goals in fast time and posted a 10 to 3 victory. Notwithstanding that shellacking a long line of fans stood outside the old Mutual Street Gardens when we returned from Hamilton at 2 o'clock in the morning.

The frantic owners of the St. Patrick's club were prepared to dismiss me on the spot but I retorted that I would brook no added interference. Just before the game began I presented a plan to the players, among whom were Heffernan, Hughey Aird, Cecil "Babe" Dye and Breen that from the outset they must bodycheck the elusive Tigers in the latters' end of the rink. And thus was fore-checking born in a case of dire necessity.

Under the plan the deadly-shooting Dye was instructed to hover in front of the defence where he would be in position to gain possession of pucks rendered loose after bodychecks had been delivered. During the early minutes of the game brilliant "Shorty" Green sped from behind the Tiger net and Breen almost demolished him with one of the hardest bodychecks ever delivered. The other players caught the signal and throughout the remainder of that torrid battle the astonished Tigers were sent sprawling in all directions, the while the capacity crowd thundered in acclaim.

"Babe" Dye, shooting with the swiftness of light, assailed that net, guarded by Herb Rheaume, with flying rubber but, probably, for the only time during his eventful career he lacked his usual deadly accuracy. St. Pats posted a 5-1 decision but lost the round 11 to 8. The following season owners of the Toronto NHL franchise changed the club's name from Arenas to St. Patrick's and lured Dye and Heffernan into professional ranks.

Reverting again to Mattawa and to its oddities and events, I remember how bitterly the Liberals and Conservatives waged stern warfare.

Overtures to voters were not uncommon. By law Indians were not permitted to purchase or drink anything that was intoxicating but agents of both parties winked at the rule.

On one occasion I entered the home of a Squaw Valley resident and there I saw thirteen bottles of potent Scotch. The householder, a half-breed, was married to an Indian and he had been 'black listed'. Thereof, I asked him how he had secured so much whiskey and he replied.

"The Conservative candidate, knowing I am a Liberal, offered me three bottles for my vote so I accepted them. Last night the Liberal candidate came to my home and when I said "I must vote Conservative because I have three bottles," he just laughed and he said "I have six bottles for you in the buggy".

"I am half Scottish, you know, so I says to the Conservative agent later, ' I am now a Liberal' but I will vote Conservative if you bring me four more bottles. That would make it 7 to 6. "So he says "Damn, you, Tom, I will get you the bottles but that will be the limit. If you raise the ante I will have you "disfranchiselled." "But he can't disfranchisel because I just ain't goin' to tell nobody how I voted."

As I, laughingly, turned away Tom, who was a carpenter, suddenly remembered that my father was the town's head scrutineer and that he ruled with an iron hand so he said, "Don't tell your father about this because if you do he would disfranchisel me and he wouldn't permit me to shingle the kitchen roof at your home and I would lose more money than this whiskey is worth."

As I used to help Tom in those shingling exercises I thought it the height of discretion to keep silent about his dual dealings with the Liberals and the Tories. And now, in looking back, I don't recall that I ever told my father about such shennanigans.

Mattawa and surrounding country was in that distant past a fishing paradise. In the evenings the rickety bridge was often jammed with bamboo pole exponents who lured fish to hooks to which were attached worms, grasshoppers or minnows. Others cast trolls into the fast-running water.

It was thrilling so-called sport because no one knew what kind of fish he would catch. In the pools near the bridge there were black and rock bass, pike, pickerel, mooneyes, perch, muskies, chub, brook trout, catfish, mudpouts, eels and occasionally a stray sturgeon.

Probably, because I was an ardent fisherman – although I wasn't an expert – I caught the two largest black bass ever landed in the Mattawa river while I was a resident of that town. On a rainy afternoon in 1905 I also caught the largest pickerel I have ever seen.

Owing to a pact made with an older boy named Johnny Burke that the catch would be divided, he having supplied the bait, I had to part with one of those precious bass notwithstanding the fact that I had caught seven, the while he had 'snared' only one, and it was of picayune size. I was only 12 years of age and when Burke demanded that he must have one of those huge bass I was broken-hearted.

Storm clouds had gathered and lightning streaked the sky the memorable afternoon that I caught that tremendous pickerel. I was the only angler in the vicinity and, seeking refuge from the wind, I descended to a pier and cast a hook into the water under the span. Like a flash the pickerel struck and in the green waters I could see that I had 'snagged' a monster.

With tenacity that pickerel fought for survival both against the current and with it. Not at any time did he break the surface but he did snap the line. Quickly, I attached another hook and he hit it again which proves that fish are sometimes 'suckers'. But he was a wily fellow, as befitted his age, and I lost him again.

Having been bereft of hooks, I resorted to a troll and as it sparkled in the water he grasped it while going full speed against the stream. That troll, held to the line and tightly knotted, withstood the pickerel's power until I had pulled that determined battler into the pier. Then with one desperate tug he snapped the line and fell among the log-surrounded rocks which, however, permitted no escape.

Only once since then have I ever seen a pickerel that appeared to be as large – an estimated 19 pounds – and that big fellow was also a nomad of the Mattawa river. As he idled in the rapids below the bridge Jack Tongue, an experienced angler, tried in vain to lure him into striking. Several lures were used, among them inviting worms dangled near his mouth, but the pickerel wasn't interested and eventually he turned and slowly vanished down stream.

In this era only memories are left of those halcyon days and evenings when we went in pursuit of those denizens of the deep. Fishermen are no longer permitted to occupy the bridge but, truth to tell, fish, in the main, have vanished to other hunting grounds.

Ike Tongue, who owned the former Timmins store, spun yarns about that glamorous past but couldn't explain why those fish vacated the river. Tongue, who launched his business career as a messenger in the Timmins Store, could, have written several books about the 'old home town'.

During one of my many holiday trips to Mattawa Ike Tongue advised me that the fish might be biting in the Ottawa river five miles north of the town. Thereof, I borrowed an aluminum canoe and in company with my wife I planned to be away until 5 o'clock that afternoon. I also made an arrangement whereby Ike would meet us on our return and drive us to Moose Head Lodge at Lake Champlain.

It was a trip of scenic beauty, with the Laurentian mountains in Quebec resting majestically in the summer sun. Notwithstanding hours of trolling we caught only two fish, both pike, and at 4 o'clock we turned homeward. We hadn't gone very far before my wife, gazing anxiously to the north, told me that a storm was approaching.

In a matter of minutes howling winds, ominous roars of thunder and a lightning-streaked sky made it imperative that the return journey must be swift. As we flashed under the big white bridge we saw fishermen as they dashed to safety. Just before we arrived at the landing place the raging storm broke in all its pent-up fury.

Rain was falling when we reached a near-by store, there to learn that Ike had not put in an appearance. I was a bit disturbed but I called a taxi cab and told the driver that our destination was Moose Head Lodge. On arrival at Tongue's Store I detected Ike in the act of 'closing up shop'.

I then stepped out of the cab and asked Ike why he hadn't kept that appointment. He gazed at me and acidly remarked, "If you look across the street you will see that a large tree, felled by lightning, has demolished my new car. When that bolt struck I raced across the street in the hope that I could extricate the car.

"It was a hopeless task and as I stood there a thunder crash shook the town. People came running from all directions and when I turned around I found that my store was on fire. And now you are asking me why I didn't meet you at the wharf!"

Ike, icy cool and generous to a fault, is probably the only owner of a large store who doesn't keep books or even notes about goods sold on credit. But his customers are fully aware that he never forgets the slightest detail. He is also resourceful in emergencies as the following factual statements will prove.

On arrival at his store one morning a number of years ago he noticed that the front door had been 'jimmied' and that a considerable amount of money had been stolen from the till. He called in the police chief who telephoned the news to authorities in North Bay to the west and to Pembroke in the east. A month or so later Ike told me the following story;

"The robbery did not unduly alarm me. This mountain town provides no escape for a criminal. If he flees to the east or west he must travel by train, by the Trans-Canada highway in an automobile, or on foot. If he goes north he would have to be aboard the Kippawa express. The only southern road leads to the vast spaces of Algonquin Park.

"Under such circumstances I did not suspect that the miscreant had gone north or south but I couldn't be too sure because anybody who would rob another in Mattawa must be completely lacking in intelligence. Several hours later I received notification that two erring brigands had been arrested near Pembroke. The stolen articles were later returned but as I do not applaud nefarious procedure I now use a lock that not even a Raffles could open."

Ike Tongue is a kind of landmark in a town of landmarks. His memory is also remarkable and he will verify every word herein written. He is one of a very few left of an old brigade and there in the shadows he clearly recalls that glamorous past when men of foresight and courage were among Mattawa's leading citizens.

Ike is a Protestant but he used to point with pride to the shining cross on the spire of the since destroyed Catholic Church and to a tall wooden cross that stood for years – but is there no more – on the top of the mountains on the Quebec side of the Ottawa river. Needless to say, his friends are legion and when he goes down that 'long, long road' tears will fall like rain in that happy hunting ground.

CHAPTER 5
Happy Hunting Grounds

In ye olden days fabulous were the fish stories told by guides and other experts. It was alleged that tremendous catfish roamed the depths of Lake Champlain which at one spot goes down 700 feet. No evidence, however, in proof of this claim has ever been produced. But it is factual that during a river drive before I was born a catfish weighing 320 pounds was killed in a log jam near Johnston's Rapids below the CPR bridge.

Around the turn of the century I personally saw a muskie, six feet in length, that had been caught by Joe Tenesco in Lake Champlain. As he crossed the Mattawa river bridge, he held the fish shoulder high and its tail hopped along on the wooden sidewalk.

Before the new high power dams were erected at "La Cave" and "Les Errabes" sturgeon in the thousands tried to or did leap those torrents as they fled north to breeding grounds. There was one gigantic sturgeon that came back annually but couldn't conquer "Les Errabes." A hockeyist named Adelard Freve once speared him but the monster snapped the line like he would have a bit of matchwood.

When they grew weary through exertion sturgeon wandered into pools near the shore line and it was then that Dave Dupont, a famous guide, trapped them in steel snares. In 1932 Dupont made a presentation of a 40 pounder to me and I as promptly dispatched it to the late Harry Anderson, then managing editor of the Toronto Globe.

Sturgeon, a la frogs, are loaded with reflex action and when Mr. Anderson used an axe in trying to split the prize, the fish, although it had been thoroughly cleaned, leaped several feet into the air. A frog, with its head removed, will survive for a long time under proper weather conditions. If one touches it or pricks it with a pin it will scratch the assailed spot with a foot. A fish's heart attached only to the head will keep beating in water. Those who doubt those statements should experiment.

In daring-do a lot of those old time Mattawans excelled. Eddie Gilligan, an athlete of ability, presented a case in point when he dove off the high CPR bridge into the onrushing waters of the Ottawa. As far as I know nobody else ever duplicated that plunge. But many others performed feats in which they risked their lives for the thrills achieved.

The raging La Cave rapids five miles up the Ottawa presented a challenge that few accepted. On one occasion four boatmen riding a pointer were thrown into the foaming trough, adjacent to a cellar. Three were drowned but the other, a non-swimmer, clung to a rock and was rescued.

A bank clerk named Douglas from Almonte was one of the first — and the few — to conquer La Cave in a canoe but when he tried it again five years later he lost his life. The "Les Errabes," another five miles upstream, was and is considered 'unrunable' but a Mattawan named Johnny Fink unwittingly proved that the feat was possible.

This accidental leap into fame occurred one evening when Fink, with his canoe anchored, was fishing above the chasm. The anchor, however, broke loose and before he discovered his predicament the frail craft had become caught in the current. Fink was no canoe expert so he knelt and he prayed and to the lasting astonishment of himself and many others the canoe sped down the chutes and safely into navigable water.

The superstitious had it that a Satan resided in the depths of the cellar called La Cave and that he never willingly gave up the bodies of the dead. Down deep below the foaming current and white caps he roamed among the sunken 'dead heads' gloatingly awaiting the arrival of the next victim.

When an Indian, who had found gold 'far in the north', agreed to guide a party to that 'Eldorade' it had been found expedient to camp over-night at La Cave. The following morning, however, those seekers of riches awakened to learn that the Indian had vanished. He never was found and legend had it that members of another tribe had drowned him in La Cave. His family, who lived in the Valley, stoically declined to discuss the matter of his disappearance.

A halfbreed who resided at the foot of the mountain rates mention in this story. I will not identify him by name because he later lost his life on the Western Front during the First Great War. He was three years older than I was and he gloried in fistically assailing me and others. On one occasion he tried to kick me off the bridge and into the Mattawa river just for the sheer enjoyment of the act.

One evening when I was watching the lacrosse team at practice he attacked me but George Train, one of the senior players, intervened. Grasping my assailant firmly, he turned him around and ordered me to kick him with force. Having made the most of that golden opportunity, I raced home but I knew that there would be a day of reckoning.

That day came quickly and with the vengeance seeker in close pursuit I scaled a fence with speed. I then grasped a long pine board and when my would be assailant reached the top of the barrier I struck him a knockout blow. He never bothered me again but in 1907, when I visited Mattawa while en route from Ottawa to Cobalt, I met him one night in the Valley and when he grasped my hand ferociously in exhibiting his strength I forced him to his knees where he trembled in astonishment, agony and surrender.

His skill with a rifle was so amazing that when he was overseas he had been assigned to the sniping or sharpshooting corps but in the fading darkness of a summer night a hidden German marksman shot him to death.

The late "Danie" Loughrin, son of the Liberal politician, was a boy with ideas. He was a fine athlete, a leader and a go-getter but he did possess an odd sense of humor. When other boys argued heatedly and threatened to fight Danie's wit impelled him to act the part of matchmaker. In sparking such goings-on he habitually placed a chip on a shoulder of one of the aspiring combatants and then dared the other to knock it off.

Having learned the hard way that a boy with a chip on his shoulder held an advantage in that he invariably struck the first blow, I notified "Danie" of my 'discovery'. He acted accordingly. During a biting cold day in 1905 a much older boy named Lessard attacked my brother Jack on the freezing Mattawa bridge.

Just as the battle began Loughrin sped to the scene but before he arrived I shoved Jack aside and struck down Lessard. Unfortunately, at that moment Loughrin espied Miss Potts, the Public School principal, struggling against the wind only fifty feet away. She happened to be en route to a dinner engagement in the Loughrin manor.

As quick as lightning, "Danie" thundered to me – and much to my astonishment–"You rowdies should be ashamed of yourselves. Fighting is most distasteful and I won't tolerate it any longer."

Miss Potts, having heard the above remarks, complimented "Danie" and opined that he was a thorough gentleman. Then, gazing at me with scorn in her eyes, she acidly remarked, " Your mother will know about this. Such rowdyism is despicable. This poor boy (Lessard) needs medical attention." Then, with swishing long skirts she departed.

I would also have 'departed' but Loughrin would have none of that. Lessard, his friend, Jack, Loughrin and I watched Miss Potts until she vanished behind a fence at Gilligan's lumber yard. Then Loughrin said, "The way is clear, Lessard deserves a good beating so give it to him Mick and there will be no interference."

The chip operation was not a Mattawa invention but in that lumbering centre it was a pronounced success for at least one of the combatants. But I did elevate it to a science when it dawned on me that it was the height of discretion to wear the chip, many of which were available on each side of the river. Years later when I was a football player at Queen's, Loughrin, who belatedly had entered the mining course, startled my teammates when he entered the gymnasium and boldly announced that he had "one more good fight left in him and would demonstrate the art" at my expense.

In a flash several players rushed him out of there and assured him that he had made a grave error. Loughrin then laughingly told them that we were old friends from Mattawa where jesting was pronounced. "Moreover," said he, "I would not deliberately deprive the Gaels of one of their regular players."

Many years later "Danie" died, a victim of tuberculosis, in faraway Arizona. While he was en route to that climate he stayed briefly in hospital in Toronto and it was there that I said farewell to one of the best friends I have ever known. With a quip and a jest he marched courageously to the end of the line. And now in a Mattawa cemetery he lies at rest with other members of his family.

Earl Neil, who scintillated in athletics in behalf of the Public

School, was a boy of great wit. His father, who had fallen on evil days financially, supplied householders with water at 25 cents a barrel. Earl was one of the first Mattawa youngsters who had had the good fortune to visit Ottawa and what he saw there greatly impressed him.

On his return he told us that in the Capital boys and even men stood on wind-swept street corners and "watched the girls go by", the while they sang "There she goes all dressed up in her Sunday clothes." In fast time we learned the words and then repaired to 'Gilligan's Corner' where the breezes were generally in full blast.

I need hardly stress the fact that the girls soon placed that corner 'out of bounds' and elected to wend their ways up the Hospital hill, adjacent to the bridge.

Hallow-e'en nights in Mattawa were "out of this world." Men as well as boys made spooky time exciting and memorable. On one occasion a buggy was placed atop the high Roman Catholic Church, the while the wonder grew how the jokesters managed to perform that feat.

"Chick" Sale would have been at his flaming best in that environment where raiding parties upset privies at every opportunity. There was one eventful night that will always live in memory. The factual story is as follows.

In Squaw Valley there lived a Frenchman who did not applaud the taking of such liberties. Thereof, he loaded a shotgun with salt, hid in a corn field adjacent to the privy and awaited the attack. With steps that were as silent as are those of Indians who stalk their prey the raiders (I was one of them) moved stealthily through the forest, charged and upset the little white house.

In a flash – and with a flash – the secreted sniper fired and Michel François, an Indian, took the full force of the flying salt in his legs and hips. Several weeks elapsed before the unfortunate victim could sit down and it was owing to that state of affairs that the sniper learned that he had hit the target.

There was another night when our party pilfered a valuable buggy from a hotel owner whose son was aligned with us in the venture. The irate owner pursued us across the Mattawa bridge, up the schoolhouse hill another 400 yards and onto a road in a forest. But, having anticipated such a pursuit we had strung a large rope across that path.

The hotelman, foaming with rage, sped into the darkness, struck the rope and catapulted into the air. On alighting he was injured and, with pursuit over, we dashed all the way to his stable, let the horses loose, dragged a large wagon to the river's edge and shoved it into the stream.

I am unable to state how that victimized owner ever discovered the answers but ever afterwards he used to gaze at me in grave suspicion. Many years passed into history before I told him one afternoon that I had participated in the frolics and that his son had been one of the ringleaders.

It was common practice to cut niches in spools, approach homes in darkness and promote a furor by rolling the spools against window panes. Such operations produce frightening sounds and they, definitely, were not appreciated by occupants of houses.

The rope trick was also given full treatment before a near-fatal accident occurred and brought such shennanigans to a halt. In this so-called trick a rope was, during darkness, placed across a front door, following which the operator loudly rang the bell. It can well be imagined that danger lurked in the vicinity.

The abandonment of such practices came after the daughter of a householder dashed to the door, fell over the rope, plunged down four steps and was knocked almost unconscious. She was a cute and gentle little girl and we perpetrators felt so badly about the mishap that the rope trick became extinct.

During the holidays in 1904 Jack and I roamed the log-strewn rivers and caught a lot of driftwood which we piled on Rankin's Point. It was legal to take any logs that had lost company stamps during jams and when running rapids. River foremen sometimes investigated but not on any occasion did they ever claim a log we had caught.

Driftwood trapped in the Ottawa river presented a problem but we solved it by building logs into rafts which we took around the end of the point and up the Mattawa river. In one year alone we caught and cut 63 cords of wood which filled the shed and over-lapped deeply into the garden.

It was mainly owing to this performance that townspeople predicted a bright future for each of us but they aimed a bit too high. We did, however, take keen satisfaction in being able to ease the financial burden shouldered so courageously by our father.

One unfortunate chain of circumstances that I will always have cause to regret occurred on a balmy June evening in 1904. Being aware that our parents would attend a ball in Harmony Hall where my father would be featured in a step-dancing role, Jack and I elected to do a bit of log-running in a Mattawa river bay.

We were dressed in our finest clothes and, as ill-luck would have it, we both fell into the stream. When we returned and found that our parents were absent Jack brightly suggested that if we milked the cow we might escape with a light reprimand.

Jack was the first to essay the task but he achieved no success whatever. I doubt that he actually aimed to conquer. I then made the test and, to my astonishment, the milk began to flow and continued until the twelve-quart pail was three-quarters filled.

When mother arrived she was amazed to learn that the feat had been partially performed. She relieved the cow of the remaining milk and after Jack told her the following morning that I had done the milking she decided with speed that from then onward I would milk the cow each morning and evening.

For more than three summers, autumns, winters and springs I milked that cow and in addition drove it twice daily in summer months to and from a pasture a half mile from our home. Never have I felt more abashed during a rather long and interesting career.

Thunderstorms in the mountains were awesome and terrifying. With fork and chain lightning flashing high up in the clouds and booming roars of thunder cracking "alerts" many people were not too proud to kneel and pray. Humor also mingled with fear as the pious and the superstitious envisaged the coming of 'Judgment Day '.

When echoes of thunder reverberated through those hills all members of an Irish family, who lived about 300 yards away, dashed to our home and hesitated not while en route. Having become accustomed to such goings-on, I seldom failed to inform my mother that the approaching visitors betokened the coming of a storm. Having performed that duty I invariably hastened to the woodshed, there to escape kneeling exercises.

I was no iconoclast – in fact I was exceedingly religious-minded – but I just didn't believe that I was about to rap at the "Pearly Gates". Moreover, I didn't expect that old Thor would exhibit any favoritism when he disgorged that lightning.

There was one afternoon that stands out in memory. The late Alphonse Gilligan, Jack and I were in a barn at Gilligan's farm when a storm broke in the west. In hastening to a door in the loft Jack lost his footing, crashed out into space and alit on his head near a huge rock.

We rushed to his aid, resuscitated him, and with a large St. Bernard dog doing the pace-setting, we hastened homeward. Then suddenly about fifty feet ahead of us the St. Bernard gasped and fell to the ground. A lightning bolt had grazed-and dazed-him but he quickly revived and as he fled he must have established the all-time record relative to sheer speed.

That St. Bernard, incidentally, was a 'character' and he learned fast. My brother Eddie had a part husky dog named Ponto which was noted for its loyalty and courage. I had trained him to pull sleighs and wagons and his speed was such that it was difficult to remain aboard those craft.

Ponto wasn't very big and never sought trouble but he would fight like a badger when cornered. One blistering hot afternoon as he lay sleeping under a large red pine tree that fronted our home, the St. Bernard gingerly approached and with one mighty gulp tore a bundle of hair off Ponto's back.

With a roar of anger and with teeth gnashing Ponto struck at his assailant, grasped him by the throat and clung to him with wolflike tenacity. The luckless St. Bernard appeared to be approaching the throes of death when I arrived and dragged Ponto away. That thoroughly frightened St. Bernard limped homeward and thereafter he could not be induced to advance closer to the scene of the disaster than the distant schoolhouse hill. Daily, and for long hours at a time, Ponto stood on guard under that pine tree and every time the St. Bernard ventured to the top of the hill Ponto took up the pursuit.

Several years later Ponto was struck by a train near the La Rose Mine in Cobalt and he absorbed a fractured back. To erase his suffering my father employed a rifleman who mercifully shot him to death in a nearby woods. I am not ashamed to say that Eddie and I wept when that indomitable pal crossed into his own kind of Valhalla.

I have owned many dogs since I was a youngster but Ponto and the one we have now, whose name is Buster, were the smartest and most intelligent of them all.

Circus time in Mattawa was somewhat on a par with a Grey Cup Day in Toronto. Those giant elephants which had to ford the Mattawa river, the lions, the tigers, the snakes and what-have-you were a combined revelation to boys who had never seen the outside world. No circus management brought in bears or wolves but the mountains and the hills were loaded with them.

There was one circus that was made more memorable because I didn't see it. I was then very young but my father, who had an appointment to keep out of town, had made arrangements whereby a store clerk would take me to the show. Dressed in my Sunday suit, I eagerly awaited his arrival and finally I saw him as he came over the brow of the schoolhouse hill.

But he turned into a shortcut lane, didn't even cast a glance at me and was soon out of sight. I felt that the whole world—or, at least, my world—had collapsed but I hastened to the Fairgrounds and there I saw a Negro dare-devil as he dove 100 feet into a large net. Several weeks later he was killed while diving at Fort William.

That diving performance in Mattawa inadvertently brought tragedy to a respected family, named Ford, in the town. After discussing the death-defying plunge Percy Ford, his brother and I decided that we would, in a smaller scale, make that experiment. Thereof, we placed a blanket six feet above the ground near a tree with Percy, the oldest and heaviest boy, elected to take the first dive.

Previous to the Negro's plunge a barker on the grounds had called to him as he hovered on the brink. "Are you, sir, quite willing to dive?" The answer, of course, was in the affirmative.

As imitators we felt that the same procedure should be employed so when Percy, who was about 12 years of age, climbed the tree and stood there on a branch the ritual was observed. Then Percy dove and, horror of horrors, he crashed through that flimsy blanket and struck his head on the hard ground.

Percy was rendered almost senseless but he was a powerful lad and he rallied, only to die from the effects of that fall, in Sault Ste. Marie about eight years later. He was one of Mattawa's most gifted youthful athletes and that tragedy left a void that never could be filled.

Hen house raids and bouillons at Gilligan's Rock were staged during nights that were dark. The culprits were never apprehended but via the grapevine we youngsters knew those answers. Late one evening, just after we had watched the Imperial Limited express speeding through the hills to the Mattawa station, Jack and I heard a woman scream "Get ready, FIRE" and from an upstairs window there came a flash and a roar of a shot-gun.

No arrests followed that episode but an Indian in the valley just happened to be loaded with shot and shell. It had been common knowledge that he had been proficient in the raiding art but the police chief, who formed a force of one, was unable to find any one in the valley who wasn't stoically silent.

Several days later Jack and I, picking raspberries on Gilligan's Rock, found fresh feathers and bones scattered all over the terrain. The feathers were of a golden hue and black and we recognized them in an instant.

Christmas eves and days previous to 1901 were longingly awaited. Six weeks—and then onward—before "Jolly Old St. Nicholas" was due to squeeze his hefty body down through narrow winding stove pipes we eagerly scanned the Montreal Star, wherein progress from the North Pole made by Santa Claus, his reindeer and his toy-jammed sleigh, plus the jingle bells, were depicted daily.

My earliest recollections are that Jack and I used to peer through frosted upstairs windows in the fervent hope that we would catch a glimpse of that jolly old fellow before he ascended the roof of our high home. But notwithstanding the shining moon and stars he came and departed without being detected.

It was late in the nineteenth century that I first attended Midnight Mass. As a general rule we arrived home again at about 2 o'clock, there to find the toys, the sleighs, the candies, the nuts and other gifts that we had, via letters. asked Santa Claus to bring. And always in ashes on the floor there were foot tracks made by that amazing Saint who on every Christmas Eve allegedly visited each home in the entire world.

Jack, being the oldest, was the first to discover that Santa Claus was dad. He did not, however, so inform me but when I was nine years of age I saw my father climbing the Hospital Hill laden with toys and that was when and how I learned Santa's true identity.

Realizing that I had made a great discovery I conferred with Jack and, acting in accordance with a theory held that 'silence is golden', he advised me to keep that information a secret. "Mary", he said, "is too young to know the facts so let her live on in a dream world of her own". "Moreover", he added as an afterthought, "you shouldn't bite the hands that feed you."

In looking back, I think it was rather miraculous that children of our era clung so tenaciously to their belief and trust in Santa Claus. The stove pipes in our home through which that mythical, and rather fat visitor crawled, with a bag full of toys, were just too narrow for such goings-on.

In election time Liberals wore red colors and Conservatives blue. The air was also kept 'blue' when points at issue were debated. John Loughrin and Charlie Lamarche, dynamic feudists, resorted to salty language and traded dire threats. It was part of the 'game'.

I recall one hectic night in the old town hall when it appeared that an Irish rebellion was in the making. Loughrin, who spoke fluently but, withal, pompously, kept rattling off promises with reckless abandon, the while hecklers made his task an onerous one.

Then suddenly a teenager who was stationed far down in the hall challenged Loughrin to a fistic duel. In reply Loughrin took off his coat and announced that he would throw out anybody in the 'house'. Roars of acidic laughter greeted this statement; the opinion being unanimous that Loughrin couldn't have beaten Old Mother Hubbard.

On the night of the election Katie Morgan, stationed high on an electric light post on Main Street, portrayed each Liberal victory by flashing a red light and each Conservative triumph by using a blue light. Katie was a staunch Liberal and it was with great reluctance that she waved the blue lamp.

The Georgian Bay canal was, of course, never built but the Ontario Liberal party did, under duress, erect a new bridge across the Mattawa river. Wooden piers filled with rock, supposedly made the bridge resistant against the river and the elements but the engineers made one deplorable error when building the span near the Mattawa shore.

Several winters later that span collapsed when the parish priest was its lone occupant. The priest, unable to escape, went down in the falling iron works and alit in the fast-running but very low icy cold stream. Thereafter, the Conservatives made this incident a stock-in-trade in pointing out that the Liberals hadn't been too 'liberal' in providing money for the erection of that bridge.

In 1905 a theatrical company composed of opportunists of no acting ability attracted a large crowd to the Town Hall. It had been advertised that a laughable farce would be portrayed. No more truthful words ever were coined. Hesitant to proceed with the venture, the company manager announced that there would be an unavoidable delay.

Unquestionably there was a 'delay' and it definitely was 'unavoidable'. Realizing that the situation was hopeless, members of that erring company placed all the receipts in a sack, fled down a back stairway and raced across the interprovincial bridge and with one exception all reached the wilds of Quebec province.

When it became apparent that many of the town's leading citizens had been hoodwinked a posse was quickly organized and pursuit of the miscreants began. The bridge, not built for pedestrians, was difficult to navigate and the man with the heavy sack got a foot caught between two ties.

Having relieved him of his ill-gotten gains a Mattawa agent ordered him to proceed north and that if he or his associates tried to bypass Mattawa by going south they would be tarred and feathered. That gentleman of the road took the hint and neither he nor his companions were ever seen again in a "Meeting of Waters" setting.

On the Quebec side of the Ottawa river a newcomer built a gambling casino of ill repute. Thereof, indignation expressed by most

Mattawans knew no bounds but some became regular customers. One lady whose husband owned a store had a niece who was being courted by a comical Hudson's Bay Company employee. The lady did not approve and she so notified the wooer.

The dejected suitor, who had distinguished himself as a lacrosse player and canoeist, was not without wit so when that ultimatum was issued, with a rider to the effect that he had been seen in the Casino where girls were an attraction, he replied;

"It is quite true that I gamble on occasions but I wouldn't know how you made this discovery unless your husband was the informant. Last night as I left the bistro I met your husband going in".

When medicine companies visited Mattawa we youngsters gave them rollicking receptions. They sold, among other things, miniature telescopes which were guaranteed to expose operations behind walls or money in vaults. Needless to say, those claims were highly exaggerated, but sales were brisk.

The barkers also averred that medicine sold would cure any ailment and that salve ointment offered for sale was matchless in erasing pain. As a side line each of several companies brought along an actor who pretended to become hypnotized, following which operations he would be placed on a bed in a store window, there to await the moment of revival.

Such nonsense went merrily on until a clerk in a moment of inquisitiveness, assailed with a pin a victim of hypnotism. With a roar that could be heard a mile away, he sprang from that pallet and raced to the nearby Ottawa hotel. I doubt that he fully appreciated that questioning sense of humor.

Movies of the heavyweight boxing bout in which Jim Jeffries knocked out Bob Fitzsimmons in the 11th round at Coney Island in 1899 were shown in the Separate Schoolhouse theatre a few years later and they did create a lasting impression. Probably, I viewed proceedings through biased eyes but I did think and still do, that the result would have been reversed if the so-called Australian Cornishman had then been in his flaming prime.

Fitzsimmons, striking like a cobra, showered the "Boilermaker" with darting leather during most of the swift action only to be knocked out when Jeffries struck him on the chin with tremendous force in the final round. In the Utica Globe I read later that Fitzsimmons had gone down because he had fractured both hands and realized the futility of continuing.

Probably as a result of youthful appraisal I have never ceased to believe that that was the most exciting and dramatic battle I have ever seen in a ring. Fitzsimmons, who was actually a light middleweight, was a revelation in regard to courage, aggressiveness and hitting power. But Jeffries was a man of iron, impervious to punishment.

Through the efforts of public-spirited citizens—men of vision—Mattawa was one of the first communities in Ontario to emerge from the lamp age and adopt electricity. Mr. Hurdman, whose son Albert eventually became the owner of the power mill at McCool's dam, was among the original planners in providing artificial light in homes and on streets that used to be continuously dark.

During the rowdy '90s there was an unwritten law that women and 'teen aged girls must not venture out onto streets after nine o'clock at night. This was an ultimatum that my father did not approve or support and he made no secret of the fact that the payoff would be dynamic if anyone dared to interfere with or insult my mother.

I doubt that any native of the town or the valley would have ignored that order. My father was both respected and feared and we gloried in the knowledge that although he never fomented trouble he would not have backed away if anyone had questioned his supremacy.

In 1904 a veil of darkness was lifted when the electric light system was extended to a corner near our home and from thence to the said home. Huge globes on tall poles provided flickering carbon lights and around these June bugs of huge size, hosts of flies and streaking bats clustered in swarms.

With bats darting in the glare, bugs, grown weary of pursuit, dropped to the ground, there to be destroyed by their detractors and attackers. Where they came from we never knew but it is factual that they had never been seen in Mattawa before the coming of the lights.

Occasionally a bat would fly into our home via an open window and then with brooms in hand Jack and I, in hot pursuit, would teach it the error of its ways. Bats. harbingers of superstitious fear, nested in church belfries by day and at night emerged in hordes seeking sustenance wherever it could be found.

The following story may, in the opinion of readers, have an imaginary touch but nevertheless it is in accordance with fact. My mother, who abhorred snakes, once reached to open the front door from within but suddenly noticed that a green reptile was wound around the knob. Hastening to the kitchen entrance she called for assistance to Jimmy Gilligan, who was passing by, and he did proceed to demolish that unwelcome visitor with neatness and dispatch.

How that snake got into the house and then climbed to the knob was a mystery that defied explanation. I seem to remember that it was a remark by my sister Mary that engendered much laughter. She had guessed that the sneaky visitor had been carried in in a plant vase and that in trying to escape he had attempted to open the door. He must have been a smart operator.

Snakes were numerous in that vicinity and especially so in the mountains but I never heard that any one of them had bitten a human. There were stories that rattlers abounded in the Laurentians but during many miles of travel and exploration I never saw a member of that dreaded species.

Maggie Costello, our cousin, once brought us two light brown rabbits from Sturgeon Falls and Jack and I took the keenest delight in training the pair. They were loaded with vim and vigor and they daringly tantalized dogs which chased them with celerity but never could overtake them.

The rabbits lived in a small house near the shed and daily they emerged into sunlight and frolicked or rested in the grass. One bright morning as I watched them in fascination a large hawk swooped down from the sky, grasped a rabbit in his claws and carried him out of sight. The other rabbit, bereft of his friend, would not be consoled and one night he vanished into the great unknown.

During the summer months, when the outdoor kitchen was in use, it was generally my task to ignite, via birch bark, the wood in the stove. However, there came a day when bark was not immediately available and I broke a cardinal rule by using coal oil which I poured from the spout of a tin can. As I drew the can away I noticed that a blue flame was attached to the spout but it died down quickly and I placed the can on a shelf . Just before I turned away there came a blinding flash which seared my eyebrows, burned part of my face and set the room ablaze. Without hesitation I leaped over a long stairs and into the yard crying 'Fire'. My mother heard the commotion and she dashed into that inferno, waving a blanket with which she extinguished several blazes. The fire, however, crept through the roof and ignited the very dry shingles. In that emergency I grasped a shovel, climbed to the roof and swept the burning shingles to the ground.

With the fight won, I didn't have to be told or reminded that coal oil must from then on be used only in lamps.

One of the most spectacular fires in the town proper reduced to ashes Gilligan's Hotel, a large wooden structure which was just across the street from the Timmins Store. It was razed with such rapidity that volunteer fire fighters were helpless to stay the fire's progress.

That hostel was never rebuilt and for many years the field where it had stood was a vacant property. On that site a monument honoring Mattawa's numerous sons who lost their lives in the two 'Great Wars' was eventually erected but now the post office is there and the monument stands just north of it near the Mattawa river shore.

During the darkness of a summer night early in the century, excitement and sorrow prevailed when the CPR telegrapher reported that the Imperial Limited passenger train and a freight loaded with cattle, had crashed head-on near Mackey's Station, east of Mattawa, and that George Morel, an engineer from Mattawa, had been killed. The news spread like wildfire and rescuers raced to the scene.

Morel, brother of the politician, was riding in the cab, en route to Carleton Place to bring back the westbound Imperial Limited. When the engine was rent asunder in the crash he was trapped and was scalded to death as he lay unconscious on the floor.

It was a night of horror and the wreckage was strewn in all directions. Trainmen with lanterns searched through the engines and cars and in that eerie glow the hissing steam from the doomed engines was mingled with the pathetic moans of the dying cattle.

The next afternoon in a little white house near the CPR bridge many other children and I knelt and prayed for the soul of George Morel, a kindly man who didn't have an enemy in that swashbuckling town. As he lay in the coffin we saw that exactly half of his face had been roasted in the torrid steam, the while the other half was unmarked.

Poor George did not leave much of this world's goods to his family but his gallant little wife bridged that gap when she opened a candy and ice cream parlor in her home. Children, in particular, became her customers and, perhaps because I was so young, I gained a lasting conviction that the ice cream she made in the cellar was the most delicious I have ever tasted.

CHAPTER 6
College Life Begins

I will not dwell further in mentioning incidents that occurred in a town where the same were a daily occurrence but later I will make reference to some of them. Following the departure of my father and Jack to the La Rose Mine in Cobalt, Mary, who was 13 years of age, was sent to Loretto Abbey in Toronto and my mother took me to the University of Ottawa.

As the train sped on through the darkened night I was entranced by the trees that looked like sentinels as we flashed past. I had seen them before during two trips made to my grandparents stone house near Wayside but now it was different because in the morning light, at 15 years of age, I would get my first glimpse of a city.

I slept only in fits and starts, the while I wondered what the new 'outside' world would be like. Eddie, who was with us, slept soundly through it all. On arrival at 7 o'clock we got aboard a buggy and while enroute to the Brunswick Hotel on Sparks street I was enthralled by the clop, clop, clop sounds that the horses' hoofs created when they struck cobblestoned pavements.

Notwithstanding drowsiness, I later stood at a window in our hotel room and eagerly watched a city awaken to activity. I was thrilled beyond expression but despair lay just ahead. Late that morning my mother, brother and I ascended the stone steps that fronted the University of Ottawa; registration followed and my higher academic career properly had begun.

Eddie, who was five years young, provided much laughter when he persisted in sliding across the tiled floor in the university hall. I joined in the merriment but after mother and Eddie had departed and I realized that for the first time in my life I was alone tears streamed down my cheeks.

Although Art Lamarche and Lenny Smith, both of Mattawa, were among the students they had come from the Mattawan side of the river and a wide gulf of misunderstanding still prevailed. Too proud to make overtures, I was a loner and quite mystified by it all. Moreover, a university did, in my imagination, appear to be far beyond my talents. But that die had been cast.

My first glimpse of a dormitory, with its numerous single beds, was a revelation. Rev. Father Dube was in charge and he assigned an iron bed to me, two rows from the aisle. Sleep did not come quickly because all around me I could hear low whispering but eventually I passed into slumber and slept until dawn.

At recess the following morning I joined a group of boys who were kicking and catching footballs. In Mattawa we had played soccer during the winter months but the only Rugby balls I ever saw were depicted on the covers of scribblers. I had, of course, heard about the mighty teams that had placed the University of Ottawa in championship brackets.

I had kicked soccer balls long distances and I thought that I might achieve the same success with the oval-shaped pigskin but I was due to absorb a surprise. I noticed that one of the youngsters could boot a ball farther than could anybody else so I asked him to let me make a test. He agreed and much to my consternation I missed the ball completely and fell flat on my back.

Raucous roars of derision greeted that mishap and, momentarily, I visualized French cadets at the military school of Brienne pointing their fingers in scorn as they held up to ridicule a freshman student called Napoleon Bonaparte. I felt ill at ease but the boy who had handed me the ball smiled in pity and remarked, "No one learns the punting trade unless through continuous practice."

That boy's name was Phil Cornellier who later became one of the greatest long-distance punters in Canadian football history. In poundage he was a lightweight but he went on to write flaming history; not the least of his achievements being that he became the rector of the University of Ottawa.

Remarkable as it may seem, I was soon allotted an inside wing berth on the junior team whereas Phil Cornellier remained aloof from competition for several seasons. Coach Rev. Father Cornellier, Phil's uncle, had spent several years in the Mattawa parish and he welcomed the opportunity to include me in the football squad.

The fourth practice I indulged in was memorable in that I didn't know the rules and didn't understand the instructions, such as when Father Cornellier said "you cover that man". My opponent, a much larger boy named Guibord, was astonished and indignant when on the next down I upset him and held him to the ground.

On arising he roared "I will hit you just once and that will be all." Icily I replied, "If you hit me you can be sure that that will be all."

Memories of those battles in Mattawa were still a too verdant green to be ignored.

Previous to 1906 and, in the main, for several years thereafter, charging by wingmen was unknown. Defending players were taught to remain in their positions, there to await the arrival of the plungers. That system held no appeal for me so I charged on every down and made myself a nuisance to ball-carrying halfbacks.

When the final selections were made the three boys from Mattawa-Lamarche, Smith and I, were allotted regular berths, the while Guibord was dropped. Those juniors participated in two games, won them both and were eventually matched to oppose a city machine called the Snowflakes. Appropriately enough, that contest was waged on a snow-covered Varsity Oval sward and neither team could make any scoring headway.

In those olden days there was a rule that permitted the kicking team to recover a punted ball if, although it hadn't been fumbled or touched by a member of the receiving side, it lay motionless on the ground. Thereof, I told our punter, Mel Rousseau, during the half time intermission that if he booted the ball into one of those snow-covered open spaces I would try to pick it up and run to touchdown terrain.

Rousseau, a talented football player and hockeyist, ignored that advice until late in the 0-0 duel and then he did by accident, propel the pigskin into a snowdrift. It was mainly owing to good fortune that I got there first and with nobody else in the vicinity I recovered possession and ran for a touchdown.

The Snowflakes, en masse, lodged a heated protest but the referee produced his rule book and provided proof that it was legal to recover a motionless ball. Needless to say, the rulesmakers were not as 'motionless' and they went on to make it obligatory that only players who were onside would be eligible to take such liberties.

In 1907 Rev. Father William J. Stanton, a native of the United

States, replaced Tom "King" Clancy as head coach at the University of Ottawa and in no time at all he did drastically change football tactics. He introduced the flying wing and the criss-cross attack. He also stressed speed and in his inaugural season he steered the Garnet and Grey to the first and only Intercollegiate Union title ever won by the representatives of that institution of learning.

Following my departure from the university in 1909 I visited Father P.S. Dowdall [my uncle] and he advised me to enroll in St. Michael's College. I did attempt to do that but I soon realized I wasn't welcome and I caught the night train for Cobalt, where my parents resided.

During the summer months in 1907, '08 and '09 I had worked in the mines where I had had several brushes with impending injury or death. It was toil that did not appeal to me so on my return I played hockey for the Shamrocks in the Cobalt City League, after working for a few weeks in the Porcupine gold fields.

CHAPTER 7
Porcupine Gold Rush

Late in December I joined the Noah Timmins assessment crew and left for the new gold fields in Porcupine. Alphonse Pare, a nephew of the Timmins brothers, who had been a brilliant football player with the Royal Military College Cadets and the McGill University Redmen, was the engineer in charge of the party. There were three others named McLeod, McCausland and Boudreau.

We reached the 222 mile post, one of the two starting points to Porcupine, on a dark, snow-driven night. Our next stop was a log shack where tree limbs supported alleged mattresses. The place was lice-infested and we did not escape their attention.

Before the sun arose the following morning we began the long 45-mile trip which was to take us over a narrow winding trail, several lakes and two rivers. We had two sleighs, each heavily loaded. Pare, McCausland and McLeod took the lighter one while Boudreau, a powerful man, and I were aligned.

Boudreau, who was later drowned in the Lachine rapids, did most of the pulling while I, using a tree limb, shoved from behind. The first eight miles offered no serious problems but the six-mile stretch across Frederickhouse Lake was agonizing. As the evening shadows approached we appeared to be losing ground instead of gaining it.

Soon the other sleigh was lost to sight but we had to go on because on that sleigh ahead were the tent, bed clothes, food and stove. Eventually we left the lake behind, crossed the Frederickhouse River, proceeded through the snow-covered forest, crossed the narrow Porcupine River and followed the trail to Hill's landing. When we were half a mile away from that resting post we found Pare's sleigh unattended near the trail.

Hungry and fatigued, Joe Boudreau extracted raw bacon from a sack on the Pare sleigh and ate it with relish. I was also hungry but not to that extent. Onward we proceeded with that sleigh, so tired that the lure of shining gold was no longer an incentive.

In darkness we reached Hill's Landing and following a repast we tried to sleep, but in vain. Lice were everywhere and they appalled me. Hard-bitten prospectors, however, were impervious to attacks and in a mysterious spirit of fun they staged lice races on the red hot stove and wagered on the results.

The next day we reached Three Nations Lake and Pare decided we would camp there overnight. The large tent was erected, brush was placed on the frozen ground and blankets were spread. Instead of assembling the tin stove Pare averred that a bonfire in front of the tent would supply all the heat we needed.

I remembered that my father had told me that heat for a tent could be generated by building a large bonfire on a flat rock before erecting the tent on the rock. Pare knew nothing about such goings-on and he also didn't know how to put that stove together.

It was only natural to expect that the five of us would lie with our heads adjacent to the entry to the tent but Pare had other ideas. Boudreau was assigned to the deepest part of the tent, Pare lay at the front near the fire and the others were in between.

With icicles clinging to our faces four of us got up and sat by the camp fire. Long before daybreak another party, adjacent to us, arose and hit the trail. As they passed us one of them asked the time. On being informed that it was 4:10 a.m. they swore lustily and openly wondered if we had lost our minds.

The following night, Christmas Eve, Noah Timmins fell through the ice in Three Nations Lake but escaped in a hurry. When we next camped in the gloaming, after having crossed Porcupine Lake, the tent was erected on a solid foundation and the stove was assembled. One such experience was doubly too much.

During the next three weeks we removed snow from veins on three claims but we found no gold. Those claims adjoined the famous Dome Mine and almost daily I traveled through deep snow to ask Jack Wilson, discoverer of the Dome, if he had located riches. His answer was always in the negative.

During the first week we were there Jules Timmins, then a mining engineering student at McGill University, came into our camp while en route to the Hollinger. Eagerly he asked if we had found gold. In reply I pointed to iron pyrites glistening in the sun but ventured no other opinion.

Jules proceeded on his way and early the next morning Noah Timmins checked into the camp. When he asked me where the gold was located I replied that we hadn't found any. Realizing that Jules had been duped, Noah pointed to a shovel blade that had no handle and roared "Take that into the Hollinger and have it repaired."

Early the next morning I tied that shovel blade to a sleigh and made the long journey to the Hollinger. Noah was amazed. Gazing at me sternly he said, "I didn't mean that you should make a special trip all the way six miles to the Hollinger just to have that shovel repaired."

At about 11 o'clock on a wintry morning during my next trip Noah said to me. "In view of the fact that you are here I want you to hold the steel which I will pound in officially opening the Hollinger." I held that steel, the while I hoped that Mr. Timmins wouldn't miss the target or hit me with that eight pound sledge.

Before returning to the camp I talked to my father, who had crossed that long trail and was busy with his books in a makeshift office. I saw him write two cheques, each for $150,000, with which Noah Timmins bought the Hollinger. I was awed and when I asked my father if the Hollinger was worth that much money, he turned from his desk, lowered his spectacles and said;

"This will be one of the world's richest mines. I venture to state that Mr. Timmins will be enriched to the extent of $200,000,000 when all this gold is extracted." My father's prediction came true – and more so.

Noah Timmins recalled his former partners; Henry Timmins, D.A. Dunlap and John and Duncan McMartin; and in quick time Hollinger stock was being sold on the market. My father kept and audited the Timmins books for 32 years.

Today Jules Timmins, the mining engineering student, is one of the world's wealthiest men.

My father was a well educated and self-sacrificing man. Although he worked for wealthy men, he was not, himself, wealthy. Notwithstanding, he sent my sister Mary and myself to universities and he never complained. My brother Jack generously contributed to those causes, the while my mother collaborated to the fullest possible extent and we did not accumulate any debt.

Riches some may have but all the money in the world can't buy family contentment and mutual understanding. Down a long, long trail, with its bitter and its sweet, I reaped no golden harvests but, a la my father, I am now financially indebted to no one.

My return trip to camp from the Hollinger would have been terrifying to any one who wasn't accustomed to the conditions in the north. I was pulling a sleigh load of provisions and when I reached Pearl Lake I confronted a sleet storm that was driven by a heavy wind. I donned a pair of snowshoes which, however, sank at every step.

Progress was painfully slow and I made such little headway that when I reached the trail on the northern shore night had come. I had a long way to go, about two miles, before I would reach a blazed tree that marked another trail, due west, that led to our tent.

Away in the distance it seemed to me that wolves were baying at a moon that was hardly visible. I carried no rifle and in those eerie shadows I prayed that I wouldn't bypass the guiding tree. My progress was so slow that I feared I had missed the marking but just when my spirits were at their lowest ebb I found that precious tree.

The raging snowfall had obliterated the trail but I lit a lantern and ploughed onward. Twice I strayed from the trail but retraced my steps and found it again. I travelled in a vale of loneliness, mingled with a bit of despair, but finally I espied the tent, wherein Joe Boudreau had kept a lamp flaring so that I wouldn't pass in the darkness.

It was 10 o'clock when I parted the curtains and staggered into the tent. "What for", asked Boudreau, "do you come so late? Sapristi; I have nevaire swear so much but I pray, too, that you're not such dam fool that you try to find this needle in the hayloft. Gawdam, I am disgust."

I answered, "I left the Hollinger in plenty of time to get here before darkness fell but every step on that wind-swept lake was agonizingly slow. The flying sleet kept crashing against my face and I was all alone out there on the lake. Neither snow nor lack of sleep appals me but not even in Mattawa did I ever see anything like this." Then I lay down and slept soundly until the dawn.

The salary I received for doing assessment work was so picayune and the lice were so numerous that at the end of the sixth week I started homeward but not by trail. In that short space of time a long winter road had been built and thus I returned on a horse-drawn open sleigh– and almost froze to death.

When I reached our home I repaired to a shed, bathed despite the biting cold and then cast all my working clothes into a garbage can. During the remainder of the winter I played in the Cobalt Hockey League. When spring came I secured employment as a game warden and a fire ranger and reported for duty at the Matheson headquarters.

Lacrosse buddies - Eddie & Mike Rodden

Eddie tackles Mike   *Photos courtesy Dana Rodden*

On the Black River – Matheson, Ontario

Winching the Saucy Kate

Photos courtesy Dana Rodden

Mike at Iroquois Falls 1913

Porcupine 1913 – The Lacrosse Gang – Mike front row 3rd from right

Photos courtesy Dana Rodden

Millie & the lion

Pipe smokin' buddies
Photos courtesy Dana Rodden

The kids of St. Anne's – late 1890's   *Photo courtesy Dana Rodden*

Mike & the Crew   *Photo courtesy Dana Rodden*

CHAPTER 8
A Ranger's Life

Jack Campbell, brother-in-law of Jack Wilson who found the Dome Mine, was the chief fire ranger at Matheson and he proved to be a friend, indeed. His task was an onerous one because in that era most rangers were selected mainly because they had friends in the government.

Campbell, a marvelous canoeist from Massey, Ontario, knew that danger lurked in Abitibi Lake, the Abitibi River, Frederickhouse Lake and Nighthawk Lake. It was imperative that only canoe experts must be sent to those 'beats' and he promptly appointed me to put applicants to the test.

That testing strip was the narrow and deep Black River and on it I made interesting discoveries, not the least of them being the fact that there was only one other experienced canoeist in camp. Most of the others couldn't tell the stern from the bow and Campbell's disgust knew no bounds.

Campbell, who had participated in the Porcupine rush, kept me in Matheson until all others had departed and then instructed me to go to the 228 mile post on the Temiskaming & Northern Ontario Railroad and there await the coming of a partner who would be one of two hailing from Toronto.

There was a stopping place at that site but it was so infested with lice that I erected a tent across the tracks. The next night Dr. Haentchel of Mattawa, Bill Richards, a minister named Morrison from Toronto and my appointed mate, a University of Toronto student, got off the train. All planned to seek refuge in the stopping place but they altered that decision when they were informed about prevailing conditions. Thereof, we all slept, or tried to sleep, on the hard ground in that snow-assailed tent.

The following morning we portaged our belongings across a half mile trail, at the end of which there was a very steep hill which reached to Wilson Lake, head-waters of Slim Creek which was eight miles in length. My partner, carrying a heavy book-laden packsack, lost his footing at the top of the incline and rolled over and over until he reached the bottom.

We had only two canoes; a government-owned chestnut canvas craft and a tiny, inadequate one which Rev. Morrison had brought along. What to do was a problem but it was partially solved when my partner absolutely refused to travel the twenty-four mile route to Nighthawk Lake in any kind of a canoe.

Dr. Haentchel's scorn knew no bounds, the while he advised that unusual fire-ranger to return to Toronto on the first train. It was then decided that Richards would accompany Morrison and that Haentchel and I would be aligned. The date was May 18th and a thin coat of ice lay over Wilson Lake.

Haentchel, an excellent canoeist, and I set the pace and opened a route across the lake. Slim Creek, most aptly named, was long, winding and narrow and it was strewn with rocks and deadheads but we eluded them all throughout the journey which ended near a high bank adjacent to a small open field.

There in anxiety we waited for about two hours before we caught sight of the other canoe coming around the last bend. On arrival at the site whereon we had erected our tent, Richards sarcastically warned Morrison not to step on the side of the canoe when he got out. But Morrison did just that and Richards was tossed into the ice-cold stream.

With my assistance he was extricated from that perilous position and his salty language would have put to shame any other person I have ever known. When I ventured the opinion that his plunge into the depths had been unfortunate he roared; "Unfortunate, hell; why this alleged canoeist from Toronto upset this so-called canoe eight times during the last six miles."

Haentchel, acting as peacemaker, advised Morrison to "go get some kindling for the fire." Morrison, shaking like a leaf, departed, taking one of our two axes. He broke the handle, returned unseen, took the other one and fractured that handle, too.

Following a campfire snack we all went to bed and soon fell asleep. It was no secret that bears roamed that vicinity but Richards had a rifle which he placed by his side. At about 2 o'clock in the morning we were awakened and heard a scratching sound behind the back of the tent. Richards grabbed the rifle but just as he was about to fire into the darkness beyond, Morrison poked his head under the bottom of the tent from outside and crowed, "don't be alarmed; it is only me."

In response, Haentchel and Richards ordered Morrison to leave the tent and throughout the rest of the night he sat disconsolately by the fireside. His sodden clothes were almost dry when the sun came and he suddenly announced that "there will be a brighter lining in the sky."

With the worst of the journey ahead of us my sympathies were with Richards. When we struck the onrushing Frederickhouse river, where ice cakes abounded, I thought we should await the arrival of the other canoe but Haentchel drove onward. Having reached the lake, however, we pulled into shore, there to await our struggling companions.

How they got there was miraculous but, having escaped death, Richards adamantly refused to cross that six-miles stretch with Morrison. So we took him aboard and soon we had vanished in the distance. Frederickhouse Lake is one of the roughest in the north but it was fairly calm throughout that day and evening. One mile out from Crawford's Landing we struck sand bars, but as bowman, I kept the canoe zigzagging over that stretch.

Night had fallen when Jack Crawford, waving a lantern, met us at the wharf. We immediately told him that Morrison was out there in the great beyond so he paddled to the rescue. He found Morrison stranded on a sand bar, soaking wet and thoroughly discouraged. But he brought him safely to the wharf.

As we sat around a blazing, friendly campfire, Morrison said "You gentlemen are beyond compare. I have in my packsack the wherewithal to chase away trouble and I will gladly present it to you."

After he had gone to the tent Richards remarked, "Never before in all my life have I so desired a bit of Scotch. It seems to me that I must have spent three hours in the water today."

When Morrison returned he hid what he carried behind his back and stated, "I am about to present to you a gift which was given to me by my dear mother. I feel sure that you, gentlemen, will appreciate it to the full."

Then, to the lasting astonishment of those he would befriend, he handed a very small jar of raspberry preserves to Dr. Haentchel.

"For heaven's sake", roared Haentchel," have you gone completely out of your mind?".

After we had entered the tent Morrison removed his clothes, donned sodden underwear and then hung up those clothes and his wide hat to dry near the fire. During the night a storm came up and when we got up in the dim light of morning we saw that Morrison's clothes and hat were covered with ashes.

The Frederickhouse River is from that point to Nighthawk Lake fast and perilous and Richards wanted no part of it in Morrison's canoe. Thereof, we took him along to Father Paradis' landing five miles upstream. There we were greeted by Sam Tongue and his son Walter, who hailed from Mattawa.

When Sam was informed that the minister was somewhere, 'back there in the current, the wind and the trough' he mildly reprimanded the unfeeling Haentchel and he ordered his son to 'bring him in alive'. Walter performed that feat and on arrival Morrison thanked one and all for the 'succor' that had come his way.

"Sucker?" thundered Haentchel, "Why, that is exactly the category in which Richards, Mike, myself and now Walter have entered. But from now on you are on your own."

"The good Lord", Morrison answered, "will protect me."

"If He does", said Richards, "He will perform numerous miracles if you reach Porcupine by crossing those portages and lakes or by taking the long 32 mile Porcupine River route."

In an attempt to produce a bit of levity, Sam Tongue told a few off-the-record stories which impelled Morrison to announce that he would proceed on his way.

Richards, who was sitting on the doorstep winding copper wire around an axe handle Morrison had fractured, dourly remarked that he would wager his bank roll that Morrison would never reach Charlie Harrington's stopping place two and a half miles away. One half mile would be across the storm-tossed Nighthawk Lake.

A head-wind and a river dotted with white caps indicated that the lake was in a turmoil. I had crossed part of it on ice the previous winter but didn't realize that it was as dangerous as many had claimed. I was due to learn the truth through experience.

Morrison, staying close to the shore line, became lost to sight after he had rounded a bend half a mile from camp. He, however, would eventually have to cross the river which was about 300 feet wide and it was owing to that state of affairs that I suggested we should not let him perish.

Amazingly enough, Richards was the only volunteer but he didn't render that decision in a hurry. Morrison had been out there for almost two hours before we started the pursuit. As we rounded the bend we espied him and his canoe bounding like a cork in those wild Nighthawk waters. Eventually we drew up beside him but we agreed that it was highly improbable he could be transferred to our canoe without incurring an upset.

After quickly discussing the problem I volunteered to get into Morrison's canoe provided that he would not attempt to paddle. "Gawdam it", said Richards, "if you perform that feat I will know why Haentchel says that you are the greatest canoeman in this forsaken country."

I instructed Morrison to sit motionless on the bottom of the canoe, placed a paddle flat on the water and made the transfer. Just at that moment a huge wave drove Richards' canoe shoreward but into low water. Charlie Harrington met us at the wharf, gazed at Morrison's extremely wide hat and roared, "What in h— have you got there?"

I do not know what occurred thereafter but later I was surprised to learn that Morrison had reached the gold belt and had become a part-time prospector. I never saw him again and I did no weeping. One like him in a life time was one too many.

A few days later I checked into Harrington's camp, there to await the arrival of a partner from Matheson. The following Friday, as I stood at the dock, "Butch" Burns, who operated a motor launch in transporting passengers to Hill's Landing on the Porcupine, checked in. And it was then that I met my new partner, Jack Bethel, a Divinity student from Wycliffe College in Toronto.

"Heavenly days", I thought, "what comes next and what will happen when this aspiring fire-ranger runs the gauntlet of that salty language in Harrington's camp?". The answer came that very evening when Bethel expounded his convictions that Church of England ministers were the best educated clergymen in the entire world.

I thanked the lucky stars that Haentchel, a Lutheran, wasn't there but George Andrews, a brilliant man who hailed from Philadelphia, proved to be an able substitute. Andrews, who later lost his life in a tent fire near Kirkland Lake, fluently, calmly and capably debated all points raised until Bethel produced a book and announced that therein could be found hundreds of names of those who had been converted to the Church of England in the United States.

"Name me one" said Andrews and Bethel, who had been thumbing through the pages, replied by mentioning the name of a famous owner of stores. In a flashing instant Andrews leaped from his chair and roared, "If that fellow was converted the miracle must have occurred after he had cheated our entire family of all its money."

One week later I planned to go to the 228 mile post, there to get a forty dollar consignment of food from Eaton's Toronto store but snow fell during the night, icy winds were howling and I decided to await the coming of warmer weather. Two other postponements followed and it was then that Bethel orated a bit sarcastically.

"When I was a missionary in the Yukon", he said, "I travelled trails in weather far colder than it ever could be here. I can plainly see that you are not accustomed to such hardships. I propose that there be no more dilly dallying and that we will make the trip (24 miles) tomorrow."

I replied, "That will be done but I advise you to put on your warmest clothes and take along your mitts. I hope that you'll enjoy that six mile route across Frederickhouse Lake."

When morning came and with it blasting winds and driven snow, Bethel had lost his previous enthusiasm but I was adamant in my decision to proceed. The river was foaming wild and I soon sensed that Bethel wanted no part of that. But the die was cast.

When we approached Crawford's Landing Bethel kept gazing longingly at that haven but I just looked straight ahead and, to the utter amazement and consternation of those who watched, we drove into that raging sea. It was tricky going down the narrow channel but finally the sands were all behind us.

Midway across the lake we plunged into the cross-winds and Bethel's large wide hat took wing and was blown behind us. Bethel, although thoroughly frightened, suggested that we should salvage the hat but I declined. In another 100 yards he stopped paddling and knelt down to pray.

Scornfully, I told him that I was a firm believer in prayer but experience had taught me that we had to paddle, too. He wept in bitter woe and, relenting, I took him ashore one mile from the river, I built a fire and, would you believe it, after he had recovered from that ordeal he said, with quivering voice, the while he trembled;

"I wanted you to pull in here because I didn't think you'd make it to the river."

"If I had known that", I retorted," there would have been no reprieve." And I meant every word of it.

The man who had so boasted about his endurance in the Yukon had been turned into a hollow shell.

About two months later we made another trip over the same route and when we drew up to the fire rangers' dock on Wilson Lake one of the said rangers, who had imbibed a bit too much of the grape, took a startled look at us and then fled into the forest. Astonished, I asked his partner; a man named Woodcock; what ailed the man in flight.

He replied;

"Following your last trip we were informed that you both had been drowned in Frederickhouse Lake. My partner, Dougherty, believed that report but I had my doubts. As you probably perceived, he is as tight as is a drum and he has panicked."

Woodcock and I took up the chase and overtook him about half a mile away where he knelt and prayed that he would be "delivered from those ghosts". I assured him that, in as far as I knew, I was still living and when the truth dawned upon him he accompanied us back to camp.

Owing to the generosity of Charlie Avery, former baseball player who as a catcher had been aligned with the illustrious "Ironman" McGinnity in Decatur, Illinois, we were permitted to use his log cabin, four miles distant from Harrington's 'hotel'. It fronted Callinan's Island and was about three quarters of a mile from Gold Island.

Nighthawk Lake, 15 miles long and eight wide, had an average depth of less than 15 feet and it was strewn with peril caused by rocks that lay just below the surface. When the storms came – and they came often – white caps could be seen for miles around. The few Indians who lived in that region remained close to home firesides when Nighthawk roared in all its fury.

I learned to know the contours of the lake so well that I drew a map which the Ontario Government civil engineer could not fault. During one vicious storm I paddled out two miles and rescued a pair of canoeists who had lost control of their craft and had been in that predicament for seven hours.

On July 4th I relayed, via telephone, the running story of the heavyweight boxing bout in which Jack Johnson stopped Jim Jeffries in the 15th round. At the end of the 13th the Matheson operator flashed the word that Jeffries had been stopped. I rushed that information along and later heard that gamblers had reaped a harvest by wagering on a knockout, which they knew had occurred.

CHAPTER 9
In the Line of Duty

One afternoon I received a message that a United States prospector named Mason W. Cashion had been drowned in the Frederickhouse River and that his floating body, which had allegedly been discovered by Jules Timmins, had been tied to the wharf at Father Paradis' camp. Bethel and I hastened to the scene where an unenviable task awaited our arrival.

The unfortunate man was six feet eight inches tall and in weight he was a giant. It was with extreme difficulty that we dragged his body up the high bank, placed it in a wooden coffin I had made and lowered him into a grave. His religion was unknown to us but Bethel conducted a brief service and I prayed for his soul.

When Father Paradis, an unfrocked priest, returned two weeks later he expressed resentment that the burial had taken place on his property but I warned him that he must not remove the body to other ground. I wrote a letter to a brother of the deceased and he replied but did not come to claim the remains.

Mason W. Cashion lost his life when waves from a passing motorboat upset his green racing canoe. Two voyageurs who witnessed the accident took possession of the craft and packsack and took them to Porcupine. I traced them, learned their address and sent them a letter to the effect that they would be arrested if they did not return what they had illegally taken.

They lost no time in obeying that order and with it they sent the following list with explanations which I have retained down the winding years.

"Mr. Fire Ranger - We did not upset dat man's canoe. She was upset bye de motor lunch. We toe heem to shore, for sure and we tie him too de warf becuz some one told us you will come. Well, anyway, what we now send back is dis. One canoo, two paddeles, tree fork, tree spoon, two plats, kup, one can beens, two pounds backon, tree loafs of breath, one cusheen, one pilow, two blankettes and de pacsac. If he have salt, peppaire, tee and sugarre she is sure melt or just sanked. Pardonne to us and pleez hexcuse."

Many years later I saw that same canoe being used as a flower pot at Moose Head Lodge near Mattawa. How it ever got there I never learned. I recognized it instantly because I knew it so well and had never seen another like it. In that canoe I had often paddled through the wild Nighthawk Lake waters and I knew it like I do the palm of my hand. Probably because they were superstitious, no others would use it even on calm days.

Many claims had been staked around the lake and work had been done on some of them, notably Gold Island where a shaft had been sunk to a depth of about seventy feet. A machine-laden shafthouse, worth thousands of dollars, had also been erected. Gold in paying quantities had not, however, been found and the mine had been closed down the previous spring.

One afternoon in mid-summer billows of smoke served warning that a blaze was somewhere in that vicinity so we hastened there via canoe and found that a fire was making headway in the leaves just below the surface of the ground. We dug a trench around the shafthouse and long after it appeared that the danger was over we returned to our camp which was about a mile away via the water route.

At 10 o'clock that night there came a great flash of light in the east and then the rising red flames that indicated the shafthouse was afire. Again we made the journey but the inferno was beyond control and nothing could be saved from the wreckage. Sparks had also started a fire on the nearby shore but we extinguished that one with no undue trouble.

One of the owners of the Gold Island property made one canoe trip across the lake that he never forgot. Two characters named McLeod, but who were not related, did the paddling. One was called Barney and the other Jack.

Storms gather quickly on Nighthawk Lake and one of them struck with that canoe a long way from shore. The mining magnate, naturally, became alarmed and he offered the opinion that they "were all crazy to be out in a sea like this." To which Barney retorted;

"I don't know how crazy you are but I have been in the Mimico asylum although I'm not even half as insane as is Jack up there in the bow."

"Turn back instantly", thundered the worried passenger, but Barney laughingly replied, "Nobody in his sober senses would turn around in a storm like this and especially so with Jack in the bow. Jack is the worst canoeman I have ever seen."

A few minutes later Barney said "Do ye see that island ahead? It was there that two prospectors got drowned last summer. They used to live on that little rock island behind us which is now known as Deadman's island."

"Take me to shore at once" roared the frightened magnate "and I will pay you each $20."

"Have no fear", Barney replied,"For the five dollars ye offered us we wouldn't guarantee we could get ye to your desternation but for $20 each we would take ye over Niagaree Falls."

Charlie Harrington closed his stopping place after the news went the rounds that better service was available at Hill's Landing. Before he left, however, he participated in one incident that could have been serious but was aligned with humor.

While he was out in a canoe looking for ducks his English cook, Harry Webb, became embroiled in a heated argument with Charlie Ross, brother of the famous hockey player and manager, Arthur Howey Ross. Charlie, who liked to joke, criticized Webb's cooking ability and, reaching for an axe, he pretended that he had lost his mind. Webb grasped a rifle, ran out the front door and, at random, fired a shot into the air as a signal to Harrington, who wasn't visible.

Harrington was sitting in a motionless canoe about a half a mile away and a few seconds later he was amazed to find that the craft was sinking; luckily, however, where the water was only four feet in depth. That blind shot–one in a million–had gone through the bottom of the canoe.

Shortly after that incident Harrington abandoned the stopping place and opened a barber shop in a tent near a falls on the Porcupine river, the while Webb became a cook in Hill's emporium.

At 50 cents per haircut, Harrington amassed more money than did Hill but the latter toiled under a handicap. With potatoes costing from $8-$12 per 98 pound bag and with butter, bacon, eggs and other essentials soaring in price, Hill couldn't make financial ends meet.

To his utter amazement he found that a bag of potatoes didn't last very long but that mystery was solved when he detected Webb doing the peeling. With great disdain for costs, Webb threw away about half of each potato before Hill made that discovery. The last seen of Webb was just a fleeting glimpse as he fled into the woods, going east.

One evening when I was in that camp a United States prospector said that he would wager that no canoeman could run the rock-laden, foaming falls and the eddy below it on the Porcupine river. I accepted that dare and made the trip with ease.

His astonishment knew no bounds and when he opined, a la Tex Rickard, that he "had never seed anything like it", I explained that I wasn't a betting man but would wager him I could go UP the falls. He regarded this proclamation as being a 'Mark Twain' joke but his laughter ceased a few minute later when I scaled that falls, turned the canoe around and ran it again.

Short-term prisoners employed to build the bush road to Porcupine provided a bit of diversion. They were a motley crew, with a penchant for getting into trouble. There was seldom a dull moment in that vicinity. Meals were served in a tremendous tent and, having inspected the same, Bethel asked permission of the 'commandant' to hold Sunday services therein.

I didn't do any cheering when I heard about this because it meant that I would have to paddle sixteen miles every Sunday morning. Fortunately, however, such goings-on were short-lived and for the following reasons.

1 Very few of the prisoners were members of the English Church.

2 The vast majority were not adherents of any religion.

3 They attended services only because they had been given no other choice.

4 Their salty language about that fly-infested country was strictly beyond the pale.

5 They didn't aim to be saved.

6 They were a rebellious, ornery lot.

The gist or the jest of that first sermon that Bethel preached will live forever in memory. He orated somewhat as follows. "Gentlemen

(Wow); I bring to you a message of faith and goodwill. You must blame no one except yourselves for what you are this day. I exhort you to do as I do and you will find eternal bliss. Come out of the darkness and emerge into the light."

Just at that moment I was standing near the door of the tent and beside me stood a quaint character who had been well educated but for years had drifted in and out of prisons. He was tougher than is leather and he proved the point when he heckled Bethel as follows.

"If ye would emerge into the light—which is just behind me—I will lead the way. I have been a robber, a thief and a bum and I doubt if I will find eternal bliss but I wouldn't do as you do now or forever more. This damn camp is no picnic but the judge who sent me here didn't state that I would have to listen to the likes of you." He turned and walked away; others did the same and the service was over.

The third Sunday that this reformation was attempted most of the prisoners broke from restraint and turned that tent into a shambles. As we paddled down river Bethel opined that they would find 'the way' but I immediately assured him that he and those road builders would have to 'find' it without my assistance.

A few days later I was at Crawford's Landing when 32 Finns and Italians staggered into camp, en route to Porcupine. Their surprise knew no bounds when they were informed that they would each have to pay two dollars to "Butch" Burns for transportation to Hill's stopping place.

Reluctantly, they agreed and they got aboard the pointer which would be towed by motorboat. Having attached my canoe to the back of the craft, we proceeded up river for about a mile before Burns stopped the engine and notified the passengers that the time for payment had arrived. It was an ultimatum that they turned down so Burns promptly cut the towing line and set the pointer adrift.

Jack Crawford effected a rescue and the next afternoon they, the wayfarers, assured Burns that the "fares" would be paid when they reached Hill's landing. But Burns knew better. He did, however, pretend that he would take that chance. I was at the helm as we went slowly upstream against the current and I wondered what the resourceful Burns would do next.

Nighthawk Lake that day was at its boisterous worst and when we struck those monstrous waves the front of the loaded pointer was lifted high into the air. Eventually, we rounded a long, low point beyond Harrington's former abode and that, owing to low water, cut into the lake about three quarters of a mile.

Then with the pointer bouncing in the white caps and the trough, Burns thundered to me above the roars of the wind. "This is collection time. Take the canoe and get me that coin of the realm" It was, of course, no concern of mine, financially or otherwise, but I gloried in the challenge and accepted it.

When I reached the pointer the enraged passengers declined to pay so I returned and reported their decision to Burns. Then without the slightest hesitation he cut the rope and left them at the mercy of the raging seas. About ten minutes later the cross wind veered sharply to the south and as it gathered momentum so did the pointer as it was swept into a journey that would have enfolded from ten to fifteen miles.

In that emergency I volunteered to return and when I did the passengers, terror-stricken, had no other choice than to produce the $64 demanded. I told Burns, however, that they were in an ugly mood and might attack us at the landing. "Like h —— they will", said Burns, "I will cut the rope opposite Hill's camp and leave the rescue to others." He did just that and as we turned to go downstream the air became blue with these cursing detractors. But Burns remained stoical and unmoved.

The motorboat trip most fraught with peril occurred in mid-July when with Burns' younger brother in command, eight miners, Bethel and I braved Nighthawk Lake at its boisterous worst. Starting from

Crawford's Landing we went up river, crossed the lake, propelled by a spanking breeze, and left four men at a mining camp.

Our next stop would be adjacent to Gold Island, twelve miles away and with night approaching and the lake a foaming cauldron we were daring fate. I was the steersman and, fortunately, I knew exactly where those numerous hidden rocks were splashed in spray.

When we emerged from the narrows the howling winds that greeted us almost drowned out our voices, the while the little covered motorboat plunged into monstrous waves, arose and fell again into the foaming white caps. Three of the workmen panicked and demanded that we turn back and that we did but only because our canoe had been cast adrift when the towing rope broke.

Burns waved me onward but in that inky darkness I swung the craft around and began the search for the canoe. Miraculously, we found it in weeds and on a sandbar. I attached it to the motorboat with two stout ropes, turned north and plunged on.

The workmen, cursing or praying alternately, threatened violence via gestures but I roared above the screaming gale, "If you interfere you will be committing suicide." Burns staggered to the front of the boat and yelled "You must be off course" but I replied. "We have just gone past that rocky reef and we will see the lights on Callinan's Island in a few minutes."

Actually, I didn't know if those coal oil lamps were still aflame because they were on the east of the island and tall trees obscured them from our view. We were then two miles out and travelling eastward on a three quarter bias. Spray flew high into the air, the while with every plunge water shook the craft and rolled over its top.

Those few minutes turned into many more before I saw a flickering light on Callinan's Island; a sight that was electrifying in effect. But some of the worst was yet to come. The closest route was to the north but it was rockbound and adjacent to the shore. The longer route was due north, against the raging winds and around Gold Island. I took that one.

As we turned directly north a great wave struck the craft and shook it from stem to stern. I glanced behind me and in the dim light I saw that the workmen were praying. I imagine that Bethel was doing the same. Those waves came on in droves, short, medium and long, and the winds whistled an eerie sound.

There is a five mile stretch eastward of Gold Island and the waves had gathered momentum as they fled before the winds. The sturdy little boat took them all in stride and at long last—it was ten o'clock—we reached the welcome shore where the workmen in the darkness would erect their tent.

I then told Burns that he could stay in our log shack overnight but he was greatly worried because he thought that we would have to retrace part of the same route in reaching that destination. I said nothing but, unknown to him, I steered the boat over the shorter rock-infested route not far from the shore. On arrival I beached it on a sandbar and momentarily, Burns suspected that we had struck a rock and were sinking.

Burns had been looking for those lights on Callinan's Island and he had become alarmed when he hadn't seen them. But they had been extinguished by Mrs. Callinan who had no way of knowing that we were out there in the storm and had been searching for the beacon that had previously turned despair into hope.

There was an afternoon when Jack Bethel unwittingly provided a bit of comedy that could easily have become a tragedy. In attempting to prove his oft-repeated assertion that he was a qualified (Toronto) yachtsman, he attached a blanket to a spar in a large canoe and ventured forth into very light winds close to Callinan's Island.

There was scarcely a ripple on the surface when he set out but Nighthawk Lake was noted for being obstreperous and it did have a surprise awaiting that adventurer. Practically without warning, the water was lashed into a fury by northern winds and they caught that craft and propelled it southward at terrific speed.

As I watched from the shore I hoped that through good fortune the out-of-control canoe would crash against tiny Burnt Island, slightly more than two miles away. It would have been akin to the finding of a needle in a haystack but it struck that target while going full speed.

I paddled to the rescue and warned Bethel that he must never again attempt to go out in a canoe alone or attempt to inflict on Nighthawk Lake the alleged skill of Toronto yachtsmen. But there came a day when via canoe he took youthful Emma Maloney, Mrs. Callinan's sister, out to see that same island.

We saw them as they vanished behind that strip of tree-laden land but they didn't reappear. Emma's mother naturally became worried so Mrs. Callinan appealed to me for help. I was also a bit perturbed and feared that they had encountered trouble in the wide expanse of water south of the island.

I made that trip in fast time, rounded the island and found them sitting on the shore and enjoying the scenery, quite oblivious to the fact that their disappearance had caused so much anxiety. What I said I will leave to the imagination of readers but I did take Emma back and left Bethel there to solve his own problem.

On another occasion two engineers took Mrs. Callinan and Emma on a berry-picking expedition to an island a short distance from the mainland and before they could return at the appointed time a storm struck Nighthawk.

Although the members of the party could be plainly seen it would have been highly dangerous for them to return via canoe. The hours dragged on and the storm became worse. Mrs. Maloney Sr. would not be consoled. She feared that her daughters would have to spend the night on that island where the engineers were camped.

It was 7 o'clock in the evening when Mrs. Maloney, who spoke little English, appealed to me for assistance. Bethel was prepared to accompany me but he would have been more of a hindrance than a help. So I went out alone, took Emma home and then returned and brought Mrs. Callinan back.

Then I issued this ultimatum. "The next time you go out in a canoe – unless I take you – you will swim or sink." Such shennanigans promptly ceased.

CHAPTER 10

He Was a Gambling Man

Jack Callinan, whose brother-in-law, Pete Maloney, found gold in Flin Flon, was a prospector, mine owner and gambler. He was a wizard with cards and, allegedly, he once sold several claims, received full payment and then regained the claims in a card game. He was highly educated and a man of great wit.

Callinan made a token wager with me that I couldn't brave every storm on Nighthawk Lake without encountering a sinking incident. His amazement knew no bounds when he lost and especially so when, instead of employing a canvas-covered canoe, I quite often used the racing craft from which Mason W. Cashion had drowned.

Canoeing in Nighthawk provided a series of thrills, not the least of them being the day that I wagered ten dollars that even with Bethel in the bow I could beat "Butch" Burns' eight-miles-an-hour motorboat in a four mile race to the Porcupine river. With the waves running wild and high, I held the craft atop the foaming crests and permitted the waves and the wind to drive us onward. We were far ahead at the finish.

I do not speak boastfully of such feats but through two summers I defied Nighthawk Lake and three years later repeatedly crossed the even more turbulent Lake Abitibi which at one point is 21 miles wide. In a storm or in rapids a Chestnut canoe is, in my opinion, much safer than is a motorboat or are much larger craft. But only those of experience should venture into such waters in a so-called frail canoe.

A canoe and a wind can also be used in escaping from mosquitoes and other pestiferous flies. Those insects will cling tenaciously to those they assail even when advancing with the wind but when a canoeist turns his craft suddenly backward they are rapidly swept into the distance.

Members of an Indian family who lived on a treeless island in Nighthawk Lake were characters beyond compare. Allegedly, the chief of the clan had conveniently managed to lose two wives in the dense forests. In 1910 he was married to a mere child but an aged squaw did most of the work.

One very hot day the chief and the squaw arrived at our camp and they were greatly surprised when they saw that, among other vegetables, lettuce grew in bunches near the cottage. When I told the squaw that lettuce was eatable she grinned in derision but she sampled it.

While we were absent later she cut all the lettuce in the garden and placed it in a potato bag. When we returned she said; "Squaw like grass very good. Me take it to the island and put it in the beans. We come back again when we want more. Thank you; whiteman sure know something."

Squirrels were a pest in our cottage. They pilfered food with reckless abandon. One evening as we sat at dinner a pestiferous red raider preened himself on a shelf. Squirrels are very wily and when hit with a rock they will feign death and lie motionless on the ground but if one is placed high on a tree in that seeming stupor he will be gone like a flash.

The red intruder I have mentioned did, however, make a fatal error. Bethel had baked some biscuits which no human teeth could gnaw and when that squirrel began to chirp his roar of defiance I struck him on the nose with a biscuit and killed him instantly.

When I told Charlie Auer that those squirrels had become a nuisance he said; "Get a box; place therein some cheese and biscuits; attach a string to the lid of the box and after a squirrel has entered drop the lid. Keep him imprisoned for two or three days; then let him loose and you won't see a squirrel around here during the rest of the summer."

I suspected that Charlie was joking but I made the experiment and when I set that squirrel free he raced into a tall tree that fronted the cottage and mingled with other squirrels. The jabbering that followed was laughable but after that day we never saw another squirrel in the vicinity. The man who had caught "Ironman" McGinnity's pitching slants in Decatur certainly knew those answers.

During a trip we made to Hill's Landing a violent storm arose and knocked down numerous trees, one of which, a high poplar, caved in the roof of Auer's cottage. When we returned we found that a large cross-cut saw, which had been hanging from the inside roof, had fallen and had become impaled in the table and partially in the chair where I usually sat.

Shortly after that narrow escape my brother Jack, an excellent canoeist, took time out to visit me for two days. He was en route to the Hollinger Mine to take charge of the new stamp mill. The morning he arrived the lake was unusually placid but it was only the lull before an oncoming storm.

On the day of his departure the turbulent waters were rolling high, the while countless seagulls looked picturesque as they casually bobbed atop the sputtering white caps. Jack didn't know where those treacherous rocks abounded so I said "I'll take the bow and you'll be in the stern."

We made the trip uneventfully but late that night when Bethel and I returned the lake was still frothing. Bethel, awed and frightened, said little throughout the journey but later in the shack he orated as follows. "I now admit what I knew long ago. You are the greatest canoeman in the business. Proof of it was furnished tonight when you never veered from the moon's rays that formed that narrow path in the water."

"Come with me" I answered "to the top of that hill near the shore and I will show you how that trick was done." On arrival I said; "You will notice that Burnt Island two miles away is so visible that you can see even the small trees waving in the wind but otherwise the lake is lost in darkness. Can you explain this phenomenon?"

His answer being in the negative, I said "The reason that you can see the island so plainly is because it happens to be in the path of the moon's rays. In another half hour or less the island will be in total darkness but those rays will still cast light on the water and will make it as bright as day. A canoeman facing the moon couldn't possibly avoid that streak of light." And a great 'light' dawned on Bethel.

We left Nighthawk Lake forever on September 15th but memories of that eerie stretch of low and raging water will never die. There were no fish there in that glamorous long ago but it was a place of charm, majestic in its loneliness. Of all those, with the possible exception of one other, who were there for any length of time in 1910 I am the only survivor. God rest them merry, Gentlemen.

In this book I do not plan to relate in detail my experiences in university life and athletics, other than what has been told about my career at the University of Ottawa. Suffice it to say that I enrolled in Queen's University in September of 1910 and that during that term I played junior, intermediate and senior football and junior and intermediate hockey.

In May of 1911 I reported again to headquarters in Matheson for fire ranging duty and thus, unknowingly, embarked on the greatest adventure of them all; the devastating holocaust that claimed an estimated 87 lives; reduced the West Dome Mine, South Porcupine, Pottsville and Cochrane to ashes and horrified the world. It was the most spectacular fire in the history of that section of the Province but it wasn't quite as "picturesque" as was the burning of the Brunston's Limits near Mattawa in 1898.

Fire Chief Joe Gagnon, who hailed from Bonfield, near Mattawa, had replaced Jack Campbell and his task was no sinecure. In truth it can be said that 'each ranger was a stranger' to him. Under such circumstances he dispatched unqualified employees to territorial 'beats' that they could not patrol.

He assigned a newcomer and myself to the Black river Abitibi route of 21 miles and he sent Bethel and the man who had panicked at Wilson lake the previous year to Abitibi Lake, which is 75 miles long and in places 25 miles wide. No graver error ever was made. Abitibi Lake forests were thus left unprotected.

Our shack was located on property owned by a mill operator thirteen miles down river from Matheson. From the outset my partner clearly indicated that he didn't elect to do any work. He knew nothing about canoeing and he didn't aim to learn.

We weren't there very long before he brought in his family and thereafter he declined to go on patrol if he could avoid it. On numerous occasions I paddled along to Matheson and return, bringing back mail and food supplies. To make matters worse, mosquitoes, black flies, sand flies and deer flies became a scourge.

My partner and family lived downstairs while I resided in the attic, to which the only access was by ladder. In preserving food I dug a cave on the hillside where ice never melted irrespective of the heat. On May 24th the weather was so torrid that it justified an Indian's prediction made that "ere the summer fled fires would turn the moon into an ominous red." Never were more truthful words of wisdom spoken.

Going up river aboard the Stover Mill steam engine-driven scow on the afternoon of July 10th I looked westward and saw that many miles away black and white clouds of smoke were beginning to roll; a sure indication that a fire had gotten out of control. I called Roy Stover from the engine room and gave him this ominous news.

Stover, a man of iron nerve, casually remarked that "the situation looks alarming for prospectors and others who are in the path of the fire", but he added no other comment. With the chief ranger ailing and on leave, I sensed that the task confronting me was a most unenviable one.

On arrival in Matheson I rushed a telegram of warning to rangers in the Porcupine district but I never learned if it had or hadn't arrived. The raging fire swept eastward, bringing destruction in its wake. The next mornin, I supervised the cutting of a road through the forest just north of the village but not all of those who participated thought that such precautions were necessary.

CHAPTER II
The Inferno Strikes

The galloping fire rode into South Porcupine late that morning, reduced the town to embers and ashes in breathtaking time, swung north and wiped out Pottsville, rounded Porcupine Lake, scorched Golden City, and then like two arrows, sped north-east and east, destroying Cochrane almost completely but leaving Matheson untouched.

When the inferno reached the northern outskirts of Matheson a companion and I were inspecting the road that had been so hastily cut by felling trees. It was a fiery furnace, made all the more awe-inspiring when it lapped up the gum-enfolded trees. It crackled as it rushed along and we lost no time in reaching my canoe on the river.

As we paddled upstream the smoke was so dense that I could barely see my companion in the bow. Trees crashed ahead of us and behind us but fortunately did not strike the canoe. When we reached Stover's mill at about four o'clock in the afternoon smoke had blotted out the sun and all was inky darkness, broken only by small sporadic fires that had assailed Monaghan's farm.

After an investigation disclosed that the members of that family were not in peril we gingerly followed the Black River to Matheson where great excitement prevailed. The village was then fairly well out of danger so that evening I got aboard the second relief train to Golden City and on it I met those indomitable men who were rushed to the rescue of their fellow citizens. Dr. C. W. Haentchel was among them. I had a duty to perform but they were volunteers and they were the bravest of the brave.

After turning westward from the main line the train made good progress before it crossed the Frederickhouse River and then came sights of desolation as we saw the smoking ruins in the forests. On each side of the railroad line and on the tracks and ties rabbits by the thousands huddled in frantic fear. They were so thickly jammed together that they looked like myriads of brown leaves that formed an undulating carpet.

The crunching of the slipping wheels as they ran over those poor creatures at low speed was eerie and appalling but the engineer had no other choice to make. In the darkness we reached Golden City, there to find that the hotel and homes were loaded to capacity. I, however, had access to the fire rangers' quarters and there I slept until dawn.

On arising early in the morning I saw that carpenters were hastily building coffins on the main street. One of those wooden boxes was the largest I have ever seen and when I asked a workman the reason why, he answered, "This one is for big Bob Weiss, superintendent of the West Dome Mine, who weighs 460 pounds. We have to build another for Mrs. Weiss and a tiny one for their daughter."

I quickly estimated that at least 200 coffins had been built but it was learned later that the number of dead ranged in the eighties. The toll taken at the West Dome was the greatest by far of all the tragedies. Rumors, however, could not be accepted at full value so I decided to visit that scene of utter destruction.

I got aboard a motor boat and when we were still a mile away I could see horses standing erect and facing eastward on the South Porcupine shore. They looked like sentinels but they did not move; the reason being that they had been roasted to death as they gazed at but refused to enter the lake. Not a building was left standing in South Porcupine or in adjacent Pottsville and not a dozen people were there when I arrived. In conversation with one of them I learned that Captain Dunbar of Pembroke had perished near a boarding house in midtown. I went there and saw the imprint left by his body in the ashes.

The road to the West Dome Mine was inches deep in ashes and burning embers but I struggled onward under the blazing sun until that objective was reached. There five miners were working overtime and in frantic haste. Nearby I saw letters and postcards lying near a tent that had been wiped out.

I picked up some of these and found that they had been addressed to Angus Burt, an assayer from Cleveland, Ohio, who had formerly been employed by the LaRose Mine in Cobalt and who was one of my best friends. His wife was the former Rose Wallingford, a Renfrew nurse, and there was a picture of her on one of the postcards.

Approaching a miner, I asked, "Where is Angus Burt?". He looked at the hastily constructed burial ground, where the bodies lay enshrouded in blankets a foot or so below the surface, and said "Angus is over there and his wife is beside him" Great tears rolled down my cheeks as I said farewell to a pal beyond compare.

Neil King, a famous prospector who had once laid claim to the LaRose Mine, lay among the dead. He and twenty-one others had sought safety in the blacksmith shop but when the fire raced across open territory and struck that refuge Bob Weiss, allegedly, had led them down the sloping shaft which was close at hand.

Ed Keeley, a former Queen's University football and hockey player, had tried to persuade them to dash through the fire to a small adjacent lake but Burt had slammed the workshop door in his face. Keeley then raced to the miniature lake, which all others could have reached if they hadn't panicked.

King and two brothers named Henninger had come up from the shaft and the Henningers had saved their lives by sucking in air that eddied behind scorched trees and stumps. With the shafthouse ablaze, King, with hose in hand, had tried to extinguish the inferno and he had died while still clinging to the hose.

Mrs. Burt, resourceful in a dire emergency, had apparently realized that all in the shaft would suffocate. It could also be imagined that, being a nurse, she had tried to go for help. But she failed. She had climbed about sixty feet when she collapsed and lost consciousness. When her body was found it was discovered that a large coal was imbedded in her breast.

Previous to that disaster Mrs. Burt's brother had drowned when, while skating, he had gone through the ice in Peterson Lake near Cobalt. They were the only children in the Wallingford family. Sad of heart, I turned away and several hours later I reached Golden City; there to be informed that Marshall Morrison, a friend and former professional hockey player, had perished on a trail as he tried to reach South Porcupine ahead of the fire.

Morrison and an old man named Mousseau, who had followed the 'Trail of '98' to the Yukon, had attempted to outrun the inferno but Mousseau, who was in his eighties, had been unable to keep pace with his youthful and athletic partner. Thereof, he advised Morrison to go on and said that he would backtrack through the fire.

I met Mousseau in Golden City and he said; "I saved my life by lowering my head into swamp water and by finding air behind the burning trees and stumps. The fire swept onward overhead at breakneck speed and then I resumed my journey. I had gone about 200 feet or so when I saw what appeared to have once been a man. From the ashes I extracted a gold watch and I recognized it immediately as having been the one owned by Marshall Morrison." And so another friend had gone across the 'Great Divide'.

Golden City was a beehive of activity when I returned. Hundreds of refugees awaited the arrival of the relief trains but weary carpenters had ceased building coffins although reports were still rife that thirty-two people had been drowned when a boat sank in Porcupine Lake. Only two bodies were, however, later recovered.

When South Porcupine was afire, cyclonic winds carried the flames at least a half mile out over the lake and it was under that fiery blanket that terrified residents sought safety in the water. The lake is deep and down well below the surface there are rocky cliffs.

The one bright lining in the sombre clouds was that Golden City had escaped destruction. If it had gone down thousands of homeless people would have been left stranded and temporarily without food. There were only enough tents left in that vicinity to accommodate comparatively few.

Relief trains that had been rushed from North Bay were loaded to capacity for the return trips. With passenger cars scarce many were taken by freight to the junction on the T & NO main line. I caught the night train for Matheson and when it reached what is now Porquois Junction there was a long delay.

While I waited at the station a T & NO special arrived and it was diverted to Golden City. The station agent told me the special would remain on the siding for another twenty minutes so I got aboard and interviewed several of those who were en route to the aid of the stricken.

When I entered one smoker I saw Mr. Wallingford for the first time in years. He had visited the station agent in an effort to find word from his daughter Rose but telegrams were piled four feet high on the floor and he couldn't read them all. When he saw me he asked "Have you come in from the Porcupine? Do you know anything about Rose?"

I knew then that he hadn't heard the news so I told him as gently as I could that both Angus Burt and Rose were dead. He screamed in bitter agony and he cried, "It isn't true. Fate would not take away from me my only living child."

I took Rose's picture from my pocket and placed it in his shaking hand and I said, "Mere words will not alleviate or lessen your grief but you must know the truth. Rose is dead. I found this picture among many others in a collapsed tent near her grave."

"God pity me", moaned Mr. Wallingford just before he fainted and fell on the floor. It was the last time I ever saw him.

When I reached Matheson I saw that its citizens were still quite apprehensive regarding immediate futurities. Sporadic small fires looked like torches that dark night. These had to be extinguished and trenches had to be dug in protecting the town.

Through eleven days and nights I slept only in snatches in Mr. Burton's home. Finally I went to bed at 2 o'clock one afternoon and I did not awaken until 11:15 the following morning. Messages sent to me were not delivered to my room, Mrs. Burton having decided they would protect me from acquiring a nervous breakdown.

On resuming duty I was told that the fiery cyclone had carried large trees high in the sky for approximately 100 miles. They were easily identified by marks placed upon them by surveyors and claims-stakers and some of them had travelled from far west of South Porcupine to Monroe township, twenty miles east of Matheson.

Matheson's two hotels and stopping places were jammed to capacity and several were there – notably George Tough – who later struck it rich in Kirkland Lake and vicinity. Long into each night they spun yarns about their adventures and among them was Harry Preston, a sourdough from Niagara Falls, who, through an accident, had discovered the West Dome Mine.

Having sold that mine for a pittance in comparison to its value, Preston, who had previously held a menial job in Matheson, proceeded to act the part of a millionaire. He purchased several suits, a $1,200 diamond ring, a costly tie pin, a revolver and other equipment that astonished all and sundry. His room in "Cap" Smith's hotel was a show place.

One evening in 1910 Chief Ranger Jack Campbell, whose brother-in-law, Jack Wilson, found the Dome Mine, wagered that he could enter Preston's room while the incumbent slept and steal the diamond ring from under Preston's pillow. Preston, who always kept that revolver close at hand, was supremely confident that the feat could not be accomplished.

About two hours later when Preston's raucous snoring reverberated through the hotel, Campbell, with the silent tread of an Indian trailer, entered Preston's room and returned safely with the ring, pin and revolver in his possession. The laughter that greeted this achievement was so loud and prolonged that it could have awakened 'the dead' but Preston remained in dreamland.

The following morning Campbell, wearing the ornaments and toting the revolver, thanked Preston profusely for such gifts and stated that they would be revered as keepsakes. Preston, looking a bit foolish, replied, "In accordance with our wager and agreement they are yours but if you hadn't been a friend you would have been riddled with bullets."

Campbell, laughing heartily, shoved the treasures across the dining room table and remarked. "This should serve as a lesson to you. Those who brag ask for trouble. Your 'fortress' had only one flaw. I would advise you to buy a lock and attach it to the door."

Matheson, with its unique characters, was the Mattawa of the north. It was a resting place or a jumping-off spot for prospectors who combed forests for hidden wealth in all directions. In the main they were regarded as 'crackpots' but some of them, notably Harry Oakes, Harry Preston, Frank Campbell and George Tough, proved that they hadn't been chasing will-o-the-wisps.

One hot summer evening as several of us sat on chairs in front of the Matheson Hotel, we absorbed a huge surprise when George Tough came tumbling from an upstairs window and landed on his back on the board sidewalk. We rushed to his assistance but he waved us aside, regained his feet and scornfully asked, "Can't a man fall out of a window without asking your permission?"

Abe Teets, who lived in a shack a few miles up the Black River, participated in some rollicking episodes but was seldom known to smile. He was a crack revolver shot and so was "Black Emma", who operated a house of ill repute on the river three miles north of Matheson. Arguments galore about their relative abilities occurred and eventually a match was arranged; the same to be staged in and near the bistro. Each hit the bull's eyes without a miss and the appointed referee called it a draw.

"That", said Teets, "I cannot accept. This is a duel to the finish and I am prepared to shoot a cigar out of "Black Emma's" mouth from a distance of twenty-five feet. I will also smoke a cigar which Emma can use as a target." Emma accepted that dare and in the cross-fire both cigars were demolished with lead.

In 1912 a representative of a London, England, motion picture company arrived in Matheson, seeking out-of-the ordinary scenes. When he espied McDougall's Chutes, which are about eighteen feet high, he went searching for a canoeist who would take that leap with the prize $500.

Crusty "Cap" Smith, a veteran sailor from Georgian Bay, owner of the Smith hotel and grandfather eventually of the late Lawrence Aurie of Detroit hockey fame, was convinced that the agent from London was out of his mind. He also knew that no canoe ever built and no canoeist who ever lived could safely leap that rock-infested and thundering falls.

Nobody questioned "Cap's" judgement but one jokester advised the agent to hand the assignment to me. When I was approached I assured the agent that the feat was impossible and that any one who tried it would be badly battered and drowned. His acidic retort need not be printed. My courage, he said, was debatable.

I replied, "It is not a matter of courage. My refusal is based on common sense. I am not selling my life for any amount of money and I aim to prove you are wrong. There is an abandoned canvas canoe at Abe Teets' farm and in it I will place 160 pounds of rock and let it drift over the falls. From below you can take pictures of that ride to oblivion."

In the bright sun of the next morning the test was made and pictures were taken by the agent who sat in an anchored motorboat in the wild-running rapids. The exposed – or developed – film showed that the canoe struck the crest with no swing attached, then it plunged into the chasm and was seen no more. Only fragments of the craft were found when I searched the vicinity. The agent caught the first south-bound train.

CHAPTER 12

Where the Waters Roared

On July 11th in 1912 a representative of the Orange Order made arrangements with Roy Stover whereby 54 celebrants would be taken to and back from Iroquois Falls, which then erupted in a wilderness 21 miles from Matheson. Stover, a man of wit, employed me as the pilot and then secretly told the passengers that I was a Catholic. The fireman was of the same faith.

As we approached the raging cataract which was 27 feet high and straight down, I sensed that many of those aboard were more than slightly apprehensive. Suddenly one dear old lady appeared at my elbow and quiveringly enquired if I knew what I was doing? I answered in the affirmative and she drifted away.

My next inquisitor was a noted anti-Catholic who had been sent to heckle me by the fun-making Stover. With vehemence he demanded that I must take the scow nearer the shore where the river, incidentally, was loaded with rocks and deadheads (sunken logs). I replied, "If others on board were like you I would vacate this scow now and let you all plunge over the falls." He retreated at full speed.

When I swung the scow around and aligned it safely close to the shore the rudder wasn't more than five feet from the brink of the falls. I have never seen passengers vacate a craft faster. It was a memorable day for all concerned and in the inky darkness of that evening, as we wended our way up the narrow, winding Black river the passengers lustily sang the hits of that era.

On arrival at the dock my stern inquisitor approached me and said "Notwithstanding the fact that you are a Catholic you are a gentleman and we all owe you our lasting gratitude." "Think nothing of it", I replied, "Pete Tremblay in the engine room deserves the orchids. When we were only 200 feet from the brink of the falls the engine faltered but he quickly brought it back to life and, unquestionably, saved many lives." He was as pale as a ghost when he swiftly stepped ashore.

It was on the Black river that I rescued Freddy Stover, the youngest member of that family, from drowning. As we moved upstream one hot afternoon with a load of logs Freddy, who was 12 years of age, tried to get into my canoe which was attached to the scow. It was an ill advised thing to do and in a flash he was thrown into the river.

A man named Buckley noted his predicament and called for help. I left the pilot house, dashed to the rear of the scow and saw that the struggling boy was about 300 yards away and was thrashing helplessly in the slow current. With time so precious, I realized instantaneously that Freddy would be beyond all help if I stopped to drain the water from the canoe.

As quickly as possible I removed my trousers and shoes, swam ashore and picked my way through dense brush while running to the rescue at top speed. On arrival I saw only a floating cap and coat where the river was 70 feet deep. I swam to the coat and dived into the sunlit stream but all became darkness and I couldn't detect anything more than a foot away.

In the darkness I moved straight downstream and suddenly my right hand touched something that felt like cloth. I jerked it and found that I had discovered Freddy. I grasped the unconscious boy by his belt and swam ashore where the bank was steep and three feet high. It was also muddy and slippery.

In frantic haste I carried Freddy up the bank and then used resuscitating measures. I prayed as I labored that God would spare the life of that fine boy and as I thought of his mother, his father, his brother and his two sisters tears came spontaneously. Actually, I feared that he was beyond all human help but finally water gushed from his mouth and he opened his eyes to find that he was still in the land of the living.

As we sat there awaiting the arrival of the scow, which Buckley had to steer, we were assailed by mosquitoes, black, sand and moose flies but I brushed them away from Freddy's face and arms in reducing his suffering.

On arrival at the mill Buckley duly reported the mishap and rescue to Mr. Stover Sr. and, turning to me, the latter said "I am glad that you got there in time but Freddy could have saved himself." Thereof, as a hero? I batted zero. During my career I rescued fifteen people from drowning and only a few of them ever thanked me.

At Nighthawk Lake I once rescued a Frenchman and a Jewish boy named Kert, who hailed from Mattawa. They had been adrift in a canoe for seven hours and they were exhausted when I reached them two miles off shore. The Frenchman was profuse in his thanks but the Kert boy has always insisted when talking to me that my brother Jack made the rescue and when speaking to Jack he has credited me with the feat. Wonders never cease.

Gratitude relative to rescues from drowning is somewhat on a par with attitudes taken by wives who are beaten by their husbands. I had several such experiences and could be an authority regarding such matters. In Matheson I knocked out a so-called man who had belabored his wife with fists. In appreciation she hit me on the head with a broom.

On another occasion when I was rangering on the Black River I became involved in a memorable incident. I was in an upstairs room when I heard a settler threatening to kill his wife. I leaped from the attic, landed on his shoulders and knocked him almost senseless – that is to say, if he had any sense. As I stood there gazing at him, his wife, also using a broom, struck me twice. The evidence was clear that I was an unwelcome interloper.

A lot of excitement was crowded into the three seasons that I spent on the Black and Abitibi rivers as a fire ranger and game warden but I will mention only highlights during the remainder of this story. Dates and years are not all of vital importance and they will be referred to only casually. Of necessity, however, there will be exceptions, à la the Dominion election of 1911.

CHAPTER 13

Reciprocity Hits Matheson

Matheson had only 108 eligible voters in 1911 but rivalry was keen and the goings-on behind the scenes flirted with the illegal. Sir Wilfred Laurier, leader of the Liberal party, had made reciprocity the main issue. Actually, few understood the meaning of the word 'reciprocity' and others didn't know how to spell it.

Previous to an address given by Mr. Gordon of the Liberal party, Bill Wheat(this is an alias), a tall, gangling owner of a pool-room parlor, had proclaimed loudly and at length that "recerperosity would salvitate the nation and make it the richest in the world." He also announced that he "would address my feller citizens and show them the terrors of their ways".

Notwithstanding such loyalty, Mr. Johnson, the Liberal whip, selected Booth's pool room, across the street, as the site for the address and there we all gathered in a spirit of fun. Following Mr. Gordon's oration – which nobody understood – I made a motion to the effect that Mr. Wheat should be permitted to express his views. Thereof, Mr. Wheat objected but under cat calls and urging he 'mounted the rostrum' and assailed the gathering as follows:

"I don't know nothing and I ain't edicated but I aim to holler that when Mr. Gordon come up the river and he said the log cutters was underpaid at $12 a month he showed that he is edicated and I say that a vote for me is a vote for Gordon and for Laurier and recerperosity."

At that moment a Conservative, who was near the door, thundered."Sit down. There are enough jackasses now in the Liberal party without having to add you to the list."

Wheat – "Jackasses, did you say? I have throwed out better bums than you from my pool room."

Heckler – "If you throw out this gentleman you will be throwed out on top of him."

Chairman Johnson – "This is a political gathering and Wheat is out of order."

Wheat – "I may be out of order but when I am in order I can throw out them criterics. As I said, I don't know nothin' about nothin' but, oh my God, how I can argee."

Heckler – "I propose a vote of thanks to this distinguished orator. Do I have a seconder?".

Bill Swift (who stuttered when excited). "I will ther, ther, ther, third the motion."

Johnson – "The thirding of a motion is superfluous."

Chief Gagnon of the fire ranging department – "I don't think that Laurier knows what he is talking about. Before the last election I sent him a letter which was written in French and he never even answered it. I will vote for R.L. Borden because he makes evaporated milk."

Wheat – "Evaporated milk ain't any good. It just ain't right. If you ask me, I think that R.L. Borden will be evaporated."

And on that questionable note the meeting was adjourned. On the main street, however, two former Scottish boxers participated in a fist fight that had no touch of 'recerperosity'. The combatants were Jim Darragh and Jim Sharp, the question at issue being that one of them had defied the laws of reciprocity by failing to pay a poker debt.

Sharp, the younger man, was favored to win but he had imbibed so freely of Scotch whiskey that science had deserted him. Darragh knocked him down three times in quick succession and on arising for the last appearance, Sharp thundered, "Jim Darragh, in my condition I am unable to defend myself but when I am sober (which wasn't often) my boxing skill is such that you couldna' hit me wi' a bag o' beans."

Wagering on the local election result got a bit out of hand and as the day of decision approached it became common knowledge that a deadlock was likely to occur. It was a well known fact that I was employed by the Ontario Conservative Government and it was also no secret that I favored reciprocity.

Thereof, one afternoon when I entered the Revillon Freres Store I was not too surprised when the Liberal whip, Mr. Johnson, asked me if I would vote for that party, I replied that I was only 20 years of age and wasn't eligible but he waved aside my objections and assured me that he, as head scrutineer, would not raise the question.

A few days later the Conservative agent sought my support and when I told him I was under-age he said, "Think nothing of it. I will not protest your eligibility."

My sense of so-called humor impelled me to cast my first vote and on election day I entered the polling booth and in record time was handed a slip by the Liberal scrutineer. Almost immediately, Mr. Browning, the lone Conservative agent in the room, said, "I would raise an objection"

Mr. Johnson, representing the Liberals, replied, "Your objection is overruled. This man has the slip and he is entitled to vote."

I voted Liberal and when the slips were counted that evening the Liberals had swung Matheson by 55 to 54. I had not anticipated such a close result but feeling was running high in the village and I wisely refrained from letting anybody know that my vote had averted a standoff and had been very costly to those who had wagered on the Conservatives.

Shortly after that unusual plunge into politics I became a pseudo lawyer under odd circumstances. The action started when a Finlander, who had imbibed too freely from a gin bottle, ran amok on the main street. He was subdued after a strenuous struggle and was confined to a box car on the railroad siding. The lone policeman in the village was absent and he had in his possession the keys to the jail and cell. Much to the amazement of those who had arrested him, the Finn escaped and his wild roars of defiance aroused and frightened many residents.

As a ranger it became my task to re-arrest and place him in a shed behind Child's hardware store. There among the oil cans, machinery, shovels and furniture he lapsed into sleep and the townspeople did the same. At about 2 a.m., however, he raised such a ruckus by yelling and pounding on the door that several of us were impelled to take disciplinary measures.

A character, whom I will not identify, assumed the role of judge and suggested that we would stage a mock trial and frighten him out of his wits. He appointed me as prosecutor, the while Norman Childs would act in defence.

Having entered the shed we lighted several lanterns and the trial was on. Childs, a very witty fellow, presented a fine case and argued that the erring Finn shouldn't be sent to Portsmouth penitentiary for more than 20 years. The Finn protested wildly but the judge ordered him to desist "under pain of having the length of the sentence doubled."

I then arose and stated that it was most unusual to place the prosecutor in such an unenviable position. I recall very clearly that I spoke as follows:

"Gentlemen of the jury and your lordship, this non-observer of Matheson laws must be made to pay the penalty for his crimes. He has prevented the people of this respectable town from getting their earned night's rest. He has threatened to kill and to maim. He is a scoundrel beyond all hope of salvation."

An interruption followed, the while the unfortunate Finn attempted to escape. I then continued; "The fact that this man has tried to escape proves conclusively that he has no respect for law and order. Thereof, I demand that he must be hanged at dawn. I recommend that that rope in the corner be used."

I have never seen a man recover from a drunken stupor with such celerity as did that Finn. He regained his senses so rapidly, in fact, that he quickly detected that the trial was a hoax. Laughing heartily we, who had been a bit heartless, released him and having had enough of that he caught the first south-bound train the same day.

Nothing much of importance occurred during the remainder of that summer and it was with considerable relief that I returned to Queen's University where I resumed my athletic career in senior football and hockey. Came the spring and another summer on the Black and Abitibi rivers.

My new partner, a young University of Toronto student named Robinson was a very friendly lad and not a word of anger was uttered by either of us throughout the summer. No fire of any importance occurred but there were incidents that kept us busy and on the alert.

In July a cyclonic lightning storm struck that vicinity and demolished hundreds of trees near Twin Falls on the Abitibi river. The rangers there were "Slim" Lougheed, a Toronto student who was later killed during the 'First Great War', and a former Baptist minister named Ed Wright.

Sensing that they might be injured or in peril Robinson and I made the eight mile trip the next day and saw a scene of grim desolation. On a portage less than half a mile long we counted seventeen trees that had been hit by lightning but it was even worse adjacent to the falls where the cyclone had struck in all its pent-up fury.

Lougheed and Wright, who had experienced great difficulty in keeping the door of their shack closed against the elements, each appeared to be on the verge of a nervous breakdown. It was a tale of horror that they told us. It was also their last season on the range.

By gradual process settlers bought tree-laden property adjacent to the Black river. An 80 acre lot netted the Ontario Government the princely sum of $40.00 and one of these was sold to Bert McClinchey, a tall, good-natured young man who soon made the sad discovery that a Frenchman named Gauthier and his large family had taken squatters' rights possession of the property.

When McClinchey reported the matter to George Ginn, the government agent in Matheson, I was requested to make an investigation. The lot was inland half a mile and when I appeared and told Gauthier that he would have to vacate the premises his wife, who didn't understand English, grasped a rifle, pointed it at me and screamed "Je guarde la place."

Luckily, I knew just enough of the French language to "guard" myself and I explained as best I could that I didn't plan to argue with a rifle. McClinchey, a generous man, did not press his claim to the property but found another and much better one farther down the river.

It was in 1912 that I first met the late Murray Glazier, a blue print genius from the University of Toronto who learned to know the country like he did the back of his hand. He supplied prospectors and settlers with the information they so direly needed and although his task was an exacting one I never saw him lose his temper.

On one occasion I took Murray via canoe to Iroquois Falls and when he stated that he would like to take pictures of the cataract from an island in the foaming water below the falls I accommodated him. I then suggested that I alone would approach the foot of the falls via the backwater and he acquiesced. He snapped those pictures – which I still have – but he definitely didn't applaud such goings-on. In the spray kicked up by the raging falls, visibility could not be penetrated even by the camera eye and Murray had ample cause to wonder how he would have escaped from that island if I had failed to return. His remarks when I rejoined him scorched that northern air.

The Black River, narrow, dark and deep, was supposed to be barren of fish but that conviction was found to be a fable when a Stover Mill's employee broke the law by dropping a stick of dynamite into the stream. No fish floated to the surface within his sight but a quarter of a mile down river and behind a bend they came up in droves.

While en route to Matheson that bright sunny day I was astonished to see numerous fish, both large and small, drifting on their backs and gasping for air. Several of them were tremendous muskies and I put one of these in the canoe.

When I reached the mill I made an investigation and learned that I was correct in surmising that dynamite had been used. I knew those signs and symptoms and I demanded an explanation. One of the millhands, whom I will not identify by name, replied; "I threw in a stick of dynamite in trying to prove there are no fish in the river and not one came up."

"Well", I answered, "you have made a monumental blunder. Many fish arose and one of them is in my canoe. I will have to arrest you but you will be allowed to take one last – or first – look at that muskie." His amazement was laughable when he saw that five footer which I immediately restored to swimming circulation.

I felt sorry for the youth and I did not take him into custody but I issued a warning that no mercy would be shown if that experiment was repeated. One month later while trolling Robinson hooked a monster which had been loitering in a bay. It, however, dove under the canoe and snapped the line.

One evening on the T & NO station platform I saw one of the oddest sights where those Northern Lights flicker. That afternoon a Matheson imbiber of spirits had pilfered a case of Scotch from a hotel room occupied by a Kentucky sheriff named Bill McClung, a tall, thin man who didn't look the part of a battler.

McClung had imported those spirits from Toronto and he was sorely grieved when he discovered that the last six and a half bottles had vanished. But he was a sheriff and he quickly guessed that the miscreant would be intoxicated. Thereof, he mingled with the crowd at the depot and soon spotted the offender.

With biting words of sarcasm McClung assailed the culprit and announced "I am agoing to whip you to a frazzle." With haste, others intervened and assured the sheriff that the whiskey raider "was one of the toughest hombres in this here district." "Nevertheless," said McClung," I must uphold law and order."

As an old Mattawan I had seen many fistic duels that ended in a hurry but I never saw any that was concluded any swifter than was that one. McClung swung, hit the target and all the lights, not excluding the Northern, went out like falling stars. It was several days later before the victim regained full use of his senses.

In 1913, following another term at Queen's University, I returned to the same "beat" as a ranger. My partner, Joe Tremblay was inexperienced and resourceful. He also had a keen sense of humor and he was a very fine companion.

Late one night as we paddled down river we could hear eerie sounds in the distance and I sensed that a group of Indians, who had collected their small government grants in Matheson, were indulging in a war dance. Thereof, I told Tremblay that I would do the paddling alone, the reason being that silence is golden—and imperative—when strangers approach Indians who are gyrating through such frolics.

Soon we rounded a river bend and there in a small open space the Indians and the squaws—wearing very little apparel—were lustily singing and wildly dancing. It was a moonlight night but the actors were oblivious to our arrival. Eventually, however, I resorted to the eerie wolf howl and the Indians, en masse, dove into their tents.

CHAPTER 14
Thrills Galore

That 1913 season was most eventful and for numerous reasons. After the spring thaw the Morrow and Beatty Construction Company, employed by the newly-formed Abitibi Power and Paper Company, cleared adjacent forests near Iroquois Falls and launched building operations on a large scale. It was a herculean task in that the nearest railroad station via water at Matheson was 21 miles away.

Machinery, horses, wagons, tents, lumber, food, dynamite and other essentials had to be taken to the falls via the water route and thus it became obligatory that only those who knew the vagaries of the Abitibi and Black rivers should be entrusted with the task. Roy Stover applied for that assignment and was awarded the contract.

The ink was hardly dry on the agreement before Stover asked me if

I would take over the position as pilot. I accepted immediately because I knew that under such an arrangement I could cover most of the fire-ranging beat daily. There were hazards involved but I knew that route so well that I wasn't at all alarmed.

We made several trips without incident but one afternoon we were late leaving Matheson with two scows, one of which was loaded with horses and was attached beside the engine-driven craft. Of necessity progress was painfully slow as we dodged around deadheads on that narrow, winding course.

Night had come before we left the Black and went wide around the Abitibi eddy that might have caused a disaster. Reefs and submerged rocks were strewn along the six mile route to the falls but my knowledge of the river prevented a mishap. We knew — or thought we did — that the last half mile to the brink of the falls held no hidden danger but we were due to absorb a shocking surprise.

Unknown to us, workmen that day had erected and sunk a small coffer dam midway in the river and the horse-laden scow crashed into it. Lights shone in the distance but they were just flickering tiny stars in that inky darkness. Roy Stover, the man of iron who had leaped the Lower Twin Falls on one of those scows, was icy cool, the while he studied the situation. Then he said, "We'll have to use the log trick in extricating the scow."

I knew what he planned to do because previously he had performed the feat in the swift-running waters below the Lower Twin Falls. On such excursions we always had a log aboard. Thereof, Stover climbed out onto the rock laden obstruction, shoved the log under the scow, attached to it a powerful rope, returned to the scow, hitched the line to a team of horses, gave the go-ahead order and in fast time the scow was freed.

Stover then gave three quick blasts of the whistle and moments later we could see lanterns being waved near the brink of the falls.

Gingerly and at low speed we proceeded along near the shore until we were about 100 feet from the foaming cataract. There Stover hurled a rope to a workman who attached it to a stump and gradually brought the craft to a stop.

A plank gangway was swiftly built via which the jittery horses were removed. They had had a very narrow escape from sure destruction and their pitiful whinnying could have awakened everybody in the workmen's bunkhouses if the wind had been blowing in that direction.

About one week later, I had a much more terrifying experience in which five lives were placed at stake. By order of the company superintendent Stover and I were entrusted with the dangerous task of bringing a scow load of dynamite from Matheson, the while another scow, carrying $18,000 worth of machinery, would be towed by motorboat.

With dynamite boxes piled so high in front of the wheelhouse that I could hardly see the oncoming river bends and with sparks flying from the flue our lone protection was provided by a canvas cover spread across the dynamite. Otherwise the trip was made uneventfully and on arrival Stover leaped ashore and attached the holding rope to a tree on an island near the edge of the falls.

Evening was approaching and I was alone when I looked upriver and saw that the motorboat-towed scow was a half a mile away. I watched it in great alarm because the cavalcade was in midstream whereas the safety-first route adjoined the southern shore. The current was very fast and I feared that the motorboat lacked the power to tow the scow to the safer southern route.

John Raynor, in charge of the towing craft, realized the perilous position they were in and made frantic efforts to extricate the scow. He partially succeeded but the gasoline engine conked out with the scow still in the current and only about 150 feet from the island. Momentarily it headed for the island point, struck a rock and veered back into the channel.

In another 200 feet those five men, the costly machinery and the scow would plunge into the sloping, rock-strewn section of the falls with no chance whatever that any man would survive. Jerry Lefevre, the foreman, who did the diving when coffer dams were being sunk, was a French-Canadian of iron nerve and he proved it when he so stoically awaited impending death aboard that craft.

Through good fortune – or perhaps as a precaution – a long rope two inches thick lay almost at my feet. I sped to our scow, removed my canoe, raced back, took one end of the rope to the foreman who attached it to the craft, returned to shore, wound the rope around a large tree and by a gradual and slow process I allowed the scow to go downstream in jerks.

A sudden stoppage would have parted that rope like it would have a bit of twine and I was well aware of the fact. Through it all the foreman calmly stood at the front of the scow, which had turned backward under pressure of the retaining rope, and thundered over and over again; "Easy boy; easy boy; give that rope the easy proper play."

In the wild-running waters spray shot high and the current seemed to be imbued with a desire to make the kill. Vaguely, I wondered why none had come to my assistance but I learned later that the near-tragedy hadn't been witnessed by anybody on the main shore. It was the most frightening and excruciating experience of my life.

With the falls roaring a dirge of defiance and four of the men collapsed in utter despair I still could hear above the roar the foreman's curt words of advice and caution. Then slowly the scow began to inch its way to the island shore and it finally reached that haven with the stern only a few feet distant from the abyss.

If that scow had gone over the cataract it would have been smashed to pieces and months might have elapsed before the bodies of the men would have been recovered far down the racing Abitibi.

The previous spring two workmen had been swept to their deaths over the southern section of the falls when the coffer dam they were on had been decimated by the ice-swollen flood that had raised the Abitibi to a record-breaking height.

According to appalled observers the unfortunate victims had been briefly seen in the rapids a half mile away but they had erred. After the new coffer dam was installed and another one was erected below the cataract the bodies of those men were found imbedded in the mud at the foot of the falls where the river had been 23 feet deep. The falls proper, incidentally, was 27 feet high above the lower river.

Indian lore has it that the falls got its name when a band of Iroquois warriors hid on the island that divided the cataract and with bows and arrows killed canoeing Algonquins and let the victims drift over the cataract. Some assert that Algonquins provided the propulsion at the expense of the fiercer Iroquois tribe.

After the two coffer dams were completed and the water was removed from below the falls, a careful search was made for battle axes and spears but none was found while I was in that vicinity. Numerous fish were, however, trapped and captured, among them being sturgeon. This discovery, however, did not surprise me because earlier that summer I had caught with frog bait a 40-pound sturgeon near the foot of the higher falls.

I gave that prize to the Morrow and Beatty Company cook and when, through reflex action, it leaped out of the huge and hot pan the 'chef' left that kitchen at a record-breaking pace.

Our 'beat' proper which started at Matheson, was twenty-four miles in length; thirteen of them on the Black River, five up the Abitibi to Twin Falls and six down to Iroquois Falls. Beyond those limits we had no jurisdiction. I mention this because of the moose-shooting incident that had no happy aftermath.

During one trip to Iroquois Falls I was told that one of five Italian carpenters had shot a moose in the rapids and had, allegedly, sold it to the construction company. There were no rangers or game wardens in that vicinity and the onus did not rest upon me to take action but conditions sometimes alter cases.

A workman who did not approve such goings-on brought word to me the marksman had boasted that "those stupid rangers will be beaten to a pulp (probably the wooden kind) if they try to arrest any of us". The workman gave me their names and I made haste to notify the offenders that they were in serious trouble.

Fortunately, they didn't know I was a ranger and a game warden so they confided in me and told me the whole story. I retorted that they would be well advised to leave Iroquois Falls immediately and seek work in Porcupine. I also offered to take them to Matheson on the scow that evening.

At 5:10 that afternoon they all came aboard the scow and my alleged sense of humor knew no bounds when they assured me that they would manhandle the rangers without mercy if they caught them. When we reached Matheson I pointed to a little red house on a hill top and told them that I would secure lodging for them within.

I knew, of course, that the huge town constable was in that 'house', which happened to be the jail. The policeman's name was Sullivan and he was taller and heavier than was the illustrious John L. of boxing fame. Having ushered in the quintetta, I introduced myself and said;

"You are now all under arrest for shooting a moose out of season. Those who laugh last laugh best."

"And", added Sullivan, "if ye protest I will knock the lot of ye into limbo."

The next morning Magistrate Hough fined them each $15.00 and when they protested he asked them what they had done with the moose. One of them replied, "We sold it to the Morrow and Beatty Construction Company."

They were then released and Hough announced that he would get Norman Childs to take us to the Falls in his motorboat because a thorough investigation was mandatory. We made the trip that afternoon and arrived just in time to have dinner, to which we were invited by either Morrow or Beatty, I forget which.

And would you believe it; we were served delicious moose steak. Hough, a bit suspicious, gazed at me and asked, "What kind of meat is this?" I replied, "It is the finest moose steak I have tasted in years."

Following that repast Hough fined the Morrow and Beatty Company $50, collected the same and assured one and all that he was a moose meat expert. When we returned to Matheson the financial spoils were split and the government exchequer wasn't given an uplift.

I do not imagine that the construction company heads appreciated the recorded goings-on but a monumental task confronted them and eventually they appealed to me for assistance after operators had failed dismally to bring in gravel from a pit five miles up the Black River.

The company superintendent, a man named White, made arrangements whereby the gravel would be transported to Iroquois Falls via two large scows which would each be towed by a motorboat. When he sought my advice I assured him that with deadheads and a large hidden rock shelf in the Black River, and with eddies and numerous rocks and reefs in the Abitibi, the undertaking was fraught with peril.

Mr. White, who did not realize that I knew these rivers better than did any one else in the world, ignored my warning and ordered the operation to begin. The first day the experiment was tested a loaded scow upset when it hit that reef in the Black River. Two days later the other scow turned over in the large eddy where the waters of the Black roll into the Abitibi.

Those scows were towed to the falls where two weeks were required to pump out the water. Mr. White began to see the light so he asked me if I would remove the deadheads from the water and mark the location of the reefs. I replied in the affirmative with the price being $50 a day.

Five days later I gave White the go-ahead sign but the next afternoon a scow upset in the Abitibi eddy and the steersman had a narrow escape from drowning. A few hours later the other scow encountered a similar fate. In that dire emergency I suggested that Ernie Sliter, a brilliant Queen's University football player, should be aligned with Roynor in towing one of the scows and that those manning the other boat should follow us downstream.

My offer was accepted and during several weeks those scows got safely through. On July 1st, however, Sliter and I took two days leave to participate in a lacrosse game in South Porcupine and while we were absent the scows again came to grief. Incidentally, Matheson won that lacrosse game, lost the next one on the home field 4 to 5 and won the other as visitors 6 to 3.

Few incidents of interest occurred during the remainder of the summer but the following were exceptions. With work temporarily halted Sliter and I went south to Englehart to attend a baseball game in which the strong New Liskeard squad was pitted against the home forces. The latter, however, could field only eight players and when they sought another Sliter did, in rare good fun, nominate me.

I took a dim view of that suggestion because I hadn't participated in a baseball game since the spring of 1909 but rather than have the game defaulted I agreed to patrol right field. "Cut" Woodward, pitching for New Liskeard, and several of his teammates were professionals and opposing them on the mound was a brother of the Mattawa boy named Kert whom I had rescued in 1910 in Nighthawk Lake.

Make no mistake about it, that Kert could pitch but his teammates didn't measure up to the opposition and after six and a half innings had been completed the invaders held a 7 to 4 advantage. Woodward, a showman, retired the first two batsmen and then mysteriously, or deliberately, walked the next three.

As I had struck out twice with the bat on my shoulder and I was coming up next, Woodward probably felt secure. Actually I hadn't even seen the speed balls he had wafted past me and neither did I glimpse the first two strikes he blazed across the plate in that eventful inning. I didn't detect the next one either but I swung blindly, connected through sheer accident and drove the Spalding far over a high tree in deep left field.

It was a four-run homer and it gave Englehart the victory by 8 to 7 but the excitement wasn't over. The visitors hotly, and without cause, protested that I was a 'ringer' and thereof wasn't eligible. Fistic battles broke out and later a riot occurred in the bar room of Kert's hotel. A fine time, indeed, was had by all.

Ernie Sliter, a flyer, who later served with distinction on the Western Front during the 'First Great War', was a loyal friend for more than half a century. He was a gifted athlete who scintillated in football, hockey and lacrosse and he was also an extraordinary swimmer and diver.

When he broke into senior company with the Queen's University football Gaels in 1910 he was only eighteen years of age but in the Intercollegiate Union senior opener waged against the University of Ottawa Garnet and Grey in the capital, he stole the thunder of the stars. As a low diving open field tackler he was one of the greatest who ever appeared on a Canadian gridiron.

Without hesitation, I would place Sliter up with the all-time native elite and thus in company with "Rufus" Ryan and Bert Stronach of the Ottawa Rough Riders; Frank Knight and "Mac" Murray of the Toronto Argonauts; Ted Savage of the Montreal Winged Wheelers; "Liz" Marriott, Don Lyon, "Cap" Fear and Jimmy Simpson of the Hamilton Tigers; and Hughey Macdonnell and Lou Bruce of Queen's University.

Sliter's fearlessness and resourcefulness were stocks in trade and he provided proof of the same one evening when through my carelessness he was propelled into the Abitibi river about forty feet from the brink of

Iroquois Falls. He, however, surfaced in a hurry and climbed upon a boom.

As he stood there glaring at me he suddenly realized that he had lost his purse and, without hesitation or a word of explanation, he dove into that deep water and miraculously recovered the purse. I might add that he was the only person I ever saw swimming that close to the roaring cataract.

Ernie arrived in Haileybury in late spring 1913. I was sitting with my brother Jack in the Haileybury Arena office when I looked out the window and saw Sliter coming down the hill boardwalk with a heavy suitcase in each hand. A few minutes later he was at the door.

Jack provided Sliter with temporary employment. A few days later I reported to fire ranging headquarters in Matheson and as soon as the opportunity presented itself I made arrangements whereby Sliter became pilot of that motorboat on the Black and Abitibi rivers.

Later that summer Sliter was transferred to Englehart by the construction company and a grievous mistake was made when it was discovered much too late that no successor could be found who could keep a scow erect in the Abitibi river. Eventually, I resigned and when both scows were upset a few days later the superintendent and his crew were summarily dismissed.

I happened to be at the Stover mill dock when White and his men appeared and in mock sympathy I asked them if they were searching for another gravel pit. They gazed at me in stoney silence but offered no explanations. I knew, of course, that they had been dismissed because they were carrying packsacks and were wearing their best clothes.

Faced with a serious problem, the Morrow and Beatty Company abandoned the gravel pit on the Black and rushed to completion at great cost a spur line to what became Porquois Junction (Porquois, incidentally, is a word representative of Porcupine and Iroquois Falls). Eight miles to the west gravel was available at Frederickhouse Lake.

CHAPTER 15
The North Again

In the spring of 1914 I had gone back for another fling at fire ranging, and headquarters having been moved to Cochrane I reported there to Chief Harry May, who was an elderly man and a forester of renown. Mr. May had ample cause to feel discouraged when he learned that very few of the rangers were experienced.

He had heard that the most dangerous 'beats' to patrol were the lakes known as Frederickhouse and Nighthawk; the Black and Abitibi rivers; the upper Abitibi River and, above all, Abitibi Lake proper, which is seventy-five miles long and at one point is twenty-five miles wide. It is divided into two parts which are called the Lower and Upper Abitibis.

Abitibi has the reputation of being the roughest lake in the world but I am no authority about such matters. It is situated at the top of the height of land and from it the waters run west and then north until they empty into the wide Moose River which flows into James Bay. The Lower Abitibi is very shallow and its width at one point is 21 miles.

Owing to the fact that the Abitibi Pulp and Paper Company got most of its timber from the forests that surround the Abitibi lakes (ah-bit-a-bee is the Indian pronunciation) it was imperative that at least one of two rangers assigned to that territory must be experienced and I was given the nod. And thus adventure loomed ahead.

It had been decreed that I must await the arrival of a qualified canoeist but research disclosed that none had been appointed or employed. All were strangers to me and there wasn't one in the party who harbored the slightest ambition to do any patrolling on the long, wide and highly dangerous Abitibi Lake.

One afternoon Chief May called me into the office and said, "the last ranger on the list is Stead Lumb who hails from Bancroft or some such place. He is a Queen's University student and you might know something about him." "Know something about him?", I asked, "Why, Stead Lumb is a Queen's University senior football player and if I searched the entire north, I could never find a more congenial companion."

Chief May - "I'm not interested in his football ability but I want to know the answers to the following questions. 1 - Is he a canoeist? 2 - Can he swim? 3 - How much does he weigh? 4 - Has he had any experience? 5 - Would he panic in a storm? 6 - Is he a forester?"

I replied, "I can answer only the third and fifth questions. Lumb weighs 204 pounds and, having seen him in football action, I would say that I don't think he would panic under any conditions."

"In that case", said May, gazing at a fly on the ceiling," you have got yourself a partner for better or for worse."

Lumb arrived a short time later and the following morning we entrained for the Forks River which empties into the lower Abitibi Lake. A construction crew engaged in building the new Canadian

National Railway line, was camped three miles east of that site. Italian sectionmen were located nearby.

An elderly man and a youngster named Thompson, who hailed from Toronto, were camped near the railroad which they patrolled. What they didn't know about fire ranging would have filled a library but this discovery was not at all surprising.

Lumb and I moved three miles down river to a shack near the lake and we soon learned that stories about Abitibi's eruptive violence had not been exaggerated. Daily I studied those wild running waves erected by wind storms that arose without warning. Lumb was no swimming specialist and I hesitated to place him in positions of dire peril.

In early morning – just after sunrise – the lake was often calm but I had noticed that when a storm was in the making the leaves atop a tall poplar tree, which was in front of our shack, would wave gently with the coming of daylight. And they waved nearly all the time.

We made a lot of trips to islands and along the northern shore and during those excursions Lumb learned a lot about the art of paddling. Lumb was, however, forty-six pounds heavier that I was and in achieving canoe balance I had to place fifty pounds of rock behind the stern seat. Such a precaution was mandatory but during lake crossings when the canoe was loaded with necessities, the middle sides of the canoe cleared the water by only a few inches.

Our shack, which had been built by a mining company, stood on the river front of a clearing that stretched to the forest about 200 yards away. On a trail in those woods we found a wolf trap that was a bit unique. A sapling tree top had been anchored to the ground and was attached to a steel trap; the idea being that when a wolf grasped the bait the tree top would break loose and lift him skyward.

It was a clever plan – but an old one – and Lumb was agreeably impressed until I reminded him that wolves were probably in that vicinity. "And", I added, "we haven't got a rifle."

Lumb, who suspected that I was exaggerating the situation, opined that he wasn't interested in wolf and fairy tales but several nights later when the moon was full those eerie wolf cries could be heard in the distance. As we sat in front of the cottage the baying grew louder and I quickly estimated that a large pack was approaching the clearing.

There were wolves in the Laurentians near Mattawa and although I never saw one they could be plainly heard when they were on the prowl. Our dog Ponto, as I have mentioned, was a husky – part wolf – and he used to keep neighbors awake when he was barking at his ferocious relatives.

"Those wolves", I said to Lumb, "have crossed the railroad tracks and they will reach the clearing in a few minutes. But they won't venture out into the opening. They are the wiliest animals in the world, make no mistake about that. From the back window of the cottage you will see their eyes sparkling like diamonds in the moonlight."

Laughing heartily at my alleged humor, Stead walked to the window and saw a host of fire flies winking in the darkness. In a way the wolves had ceased to bay and Stead was feeling gay. But he changed that tune quickly when I said, "Those lights that do not blink are wolves' eyes that shine in the moon's rays. The wolves see this cottage and they suspect that there is safety in silence."

Eventually the marauders fled northward and as they thundered onward they again began to bay and, lo and behold, from the nearest island, which was only about thirty feet from the main shore, there came a lone reply that sounded like an echo.

"And what on earth is that?" asked Lumb. "It is", I replied, "the baying of a loner who must have been left stranded on that island when the ice went out. Wolves, believe it or not, are not too keen about entering water. When a litter is born there is generally at least one that will noisily lap water and the mother immediately destroys it. It is the dog member in the family and its barking might draw hunters to the kill."

Nightly when the moon shone brightly in the sky that wolf roared in loneliness and he became a nuisance. The island was narrow and a half mile in length but we never found even a trace of his 'wolfship'. He was there and he, no doubt, saw us but he was too shrewd to emerge from hiding.

CHAPTER 16
I Meet Roza Brown

Late one afternoon as we continued the canoe patrol we were astonished to see that a woman prospector and a guide were sitting near two tents at the south end of the island. "Well what do you know?" said Lumb, "The wolf seems to have company unless my eyes deceive me."

The strangers waved to us and when we landed the lady said "I am Mrs. Roza Brown and this gentleman is my guide. I am prospecting for gold."

"Well, Roza", I answered, "I do not imagine that you will find gold in paying quantities in this district. Several claims have been carefully examined and Noah Timmins spent $100,000 when a shaft was sunk on Mosher Island. The lake and surrounding territory have been abandoned."

Roza, a chain-smoking character who in search of gold had come to this country from Budapest, Hungary, had been an owner of a boarding house in Swastika when in 1911 she advised the late Harry Oakes, who was then worth $2.65, to seek the shining riches at Kirkland Lake. Oakes took the hint, aligned himself with the Tough brothers – George, Tom, Bob and Jack – and staked the Tough-Oakes mine on property that the Burrows brothers, who were mining engineers, lost because they had failed to do the assessment work.

In 'The Life and Death of Harry Oakes' it is written that Roza Brown was strikingly ugly, did not smell too good, always wore rubber boots and a fur coat and was followed everywhere she went by snarling dogs. She was in her late fifties when she met Harry Oakes who asked her "What are my chances in Ontario?"

"Why don't you look around and see?" asked Roza, "There's gold around, my friend."

"Well, why hasn't it been found?" asked Oakes.

"Gold", laughed Roza, "has a mind of its own. Gold is a woman. All the gold in the world is waiting for just one thing, for the right man to find it."

When I met Roza at Abitibi Lake three years later she was in her early sixties and although she didn't qualify for entry in a beauty contest she wasn't as ugly as has been charged. She was wearing high boots and a short skirt but I didn't see an overcoat in the vicinity. No dogs snarled at her and the wolf I sought to find was probably hiding in a cave.

"You young 'uns", Roza said, "shouldn't go gallivanting around on a lake like this 'un. There are safer places in the world."

"I believe you", I replied, "and perhaps one of those safer places could be a boarding house down around Swastika where the jokes weren't all on Oakes. Roza, my dear, have no fear, I would wager your money, which I haven't got, that I can cross Abitibi Lake every day in the summer."

"You may", said Lumb," cross it every day or night in the summer but you won't be crossing it with me."

Roza and her taciturn guide left Abitibi Lake the next morning and I never saw her again. She died when she was ninety-five years of age.

While on patrol one morning we were astonished to see hundreds of suckers spawning near an island shore. We pulled thirty-two of them into the canoe and later sold them for three dollars to Italian section hands. They thought that they had driven a shrewd bargain but when they tried to boil them they found that the buyers had replaced the 'suckers'.

Those victimized protested volubly and one of them, with axe in hand, roared, "I will keel ayou eef you don't back our monee geev."

"If you kill us", I replied, "I will have to arrest you. But don't get so excited. It was just a joke and we have brought back your money." Appeasement, unquestionably, was the height of valor.

Each night the trainmen, some of whom had been dismissed from regular service only to be re-employed by railroad building contractors, played poker under lantern light in a tumbledown car on the siding. Lumb occasionally participated in those games for diversion but I remained a looker-on, which was fortunate.

Stakes were fairly high and one evening I detected a huge engineer, who weighed about 300 pounds, stacking the deck. As the raises mounted all the participants with the exception of Lumb, who held four sixes, withdrew. Lumb finally called and the engineer produced four nines and reached for the 'pot'.

But I reached first and shoved those numerous quarters into Lumb's keeping. As a bystander I was not eligible to intervene and the engineer, whom I will call Hay, threatened to attack me. I accepted his challenge and outside amid the shadows and the dim lantern lighting we waged a duel that I won when the engineer tripped over a rail and hit his head on a stone.

Shortly after that incident we crossed the lake for the first time and took up residence for two weeks in an abandoned camp near the Narrows which divide the upper and lower lakes. There we stored food supplies before departing for Machessney's Portage on the long point that extends north and far out into the Upper Abitibi.

There are three small lakes on the point and an investigation disclosed that no canoeist had visited them in many years. Small alders had grown in the creek that leads to the first lake, in which we caught pike of very greenish hue. It was not without difficulty that we propelled the canoe between and around those thickly-growing alders.

The second lake was more accessible and there by trolling we caught the usual kind of grass pike. We shoved on to the last one, which was long and narrow and held water that appeared to be rusted and had a dark, brownish tinge. After testing it we reached the conclusion that it was barren of fish but when I started to pull in the line a denizen of those lonely waters struck it and the battle was on.

That enraged or fear-stricken fish made the waters sizzle as he struggled to escape. When he wasn't swimming swiftly in any one direction he kept leaping high into the air and in the bright sun he shook and shed water globules that looked like shining diamonds.

As he fought on and I kept pulling in the line the canoe, not the fish, did the moving. When we got close enough I saw a fish, the like of which I had never glimpsed before and haven't seen since. He was a darker brown than was the leaf-filled lake and he was thick and comparatively short. He didn't look the part but he was a pike.

I fried the fish that evening, the while I anticipated that we would have a feast, but that pike meat was the toughest I have ever eaten. I suggested to Lumb that the pike (not Lumb) must have been around at the time of the flood but Lumb disagreed and guessed that it wasn't more than 1,000 years old. Needless to say, we never returned to that particular lake.

There was another lake on the portage and it was held in dread by superstitious Indians. In trying to discover its depth we sank a rock attached to a rope 200 feet long and failed to reach bottom. It was loaded with mud and mire that could be seen from the surface and pike were there in abundance.

Late in June we recrossed the lake on which hardly a ripple appeared. We were en route to the 'steel' (the railway) there to get supplies we had ordered in Toronto. Incidentally, the cost for eatables during an entire summer did not exceed $40.00 for the both of us. Fish and berries at no cost at all eased financial expenditures.

The rangers at the Forks river, an ill-assorted pair, were in a 'grumpy' mood. One happened to be too old and the other, Thompson, too young. Neither was a cook and relations were a bit strained. Lumb, a jolly fellow, suggested that a game of cards might help to ease the tensions but it did just the reverse.

One word led to another and Thompson erred by challenging Lumb to a fistic duel. He was unaware that Lumb was one of the strongest football players in the Intercollegiate Union. Thereof, Lumb picked Thompson up bodily, carried him to the river and threw him in. As a cooling-off process that action has never been excelled.

I then volunteered to cook the evening meal and I proceeded to 'invent' a dish that was composed of the following ingredients, placed in layers. Macaroni, cheese, onions and canned tomatoes with salt, pepper and butter added. The other rangers, suspecting the worst, gingerly partook of that remarkable concoction, found it deliciously appetizing and, with my assistance, consumed the entire treat.

Late that night we paddled down river in that cold northern air which reeked of frost, the while the constant drumming of mosquitoes produced an eerie roar that sounded like a band. The moon shining brightly in that crispy air portrayed Abitibi Lake at its picturesque best.

The following morning, however, the lake was at its turbulent worst and day after day the winds howled and screamed their doleful tune of defiance. For diversion we did a bit of fishing and found that bass, pike and pickerel were numerous in an adjoining bay and also in a narrow channel near the river.

There came a morning when Lumb, looking eastward, reported that smoke was rising high in the distance. I joined him in a hurry and estimated that a fire was burning many miles away on the north side of the Upper Abitibi. I guessed correctly that it was on property owned by the Abitibi Company and that the onus rested with that organization to subdue it.

The Abitibi Power and Paper Company's shanties were situated on the south side of the Lower Abitibi Lake about seventeen miles from our camp. The company had two motorboats and a steamer that was seventy-five feet long. Under such circumstances I felt that Superintendent Hennessey and his foreman, John Carmichael and Joe Lafraniere, should rush fire-fighters to the scene of the blaze.

With the lake in an uproar every day, I declined to risk two lives and I also knew full well that not even hundreds of men could stop a fire after it had reached cyclonic proportions. Early on the morning of the third day of the fire Chief May reached our camp and asked us why we hadn't gone to the upper lake. I replied "Are you suggesting that we should commit suicide. The lake is rough now but you should see it in the afternoon."

Reluctantly, Chief May accepted that delay but when we got up at sunrise he said "The lake is as calm as glass so I am ordering you to proceed."

I walked to the door, glanced at the poplar tree and remarked, "A storm is brewing in the east and unless I am mistaken it will strike the lake at about ten o'clock this morning. I would also predict that in a few hours smoke on the lake will obliterate even that little island which is only half a mile from here."

The chief, agitated because of the fire, seemed to forget that even under the most favorable conditions at least twelve hours would elapse before we could reach the burning forest which was about sixty-miles south-east. He was not a canoe specialist but he was in command so I cast the die and said, "We will leave here at sunrise but in the meantime I would advise you to rush word via motorboat from Lowbush to Hennessey and tell him that the onus rests with him to fight the fire."

We were up at daybreak, took a hurried breakfast and were soon on our way, sans a tent or provisions. We did, however, take along two blankets, a small bag of flour with which we could make bannock if we had to seek shelter on the island, one packsack loaded with clothes and another with dishes, pans and other cooking essentials.

We were five miles offshore when we saw that wind-driven heavy smoke from the east was descending on the lake. In a matter of minutes vision was blotted out and I couldn't see a landmark in any direction. In our planned path there were several islands but to the right only the Mosher Mine islet lay in a water wilderness of approximately a hundred square miles.

With no landmark in sight Lumb's superior weight veered the canoe off course and eventually we became lost in those wide open spaces. Throughout that long day we wandered in a very wide circle but just as evening approached we were both truly thankful when we espied a small island just ahead of us.

On landing that rock-strewn and treeless haven looked familiar but we had never been on it and had no way of knowing just where it was situated. We lit a fire, baked bannock, ate some berries and fell soundly asleep with the moon and stars shining brightly in the heavens. A slight rain fell during the night but it did not disturb our slumber.

On awakening I gazed northward and made the startling discovery that after having paddled continuously for about fourteen hours we were just a half mile away from our starting point on the Forks river. We returned to the camp and got some butter and tea and then hit the water route again.

We paddled at top speed in an effort to jump the gap to the Narrows seventeen miles away before the smoke could assail us again. But we failed and when an island loomed up in the gloom I decided we would stay there overnight. On arrival, however, we found that there was no place to land so we continued on and luckily located an islet about midway in the lake. The waves were rolling mountainous high and over that rock-bound ledge but we landed safely.

I placed the canoe high in a tree and Lumb attached the two packsacks to a stout pine. We then cut down a lot of balsam branches and placed them thickly over a blanket erected like a tent. We next cut some small trees with which we made a bed about a foot above the ground. Throughout the night and during the next three days and nights we were held captive in loneliness, the while water rolled beneath the bed.

During the fourth night fork and chain lightning streaked the skies and a slight rain fell. As we lay there in our makeshift tent I told Lumb that come what may, we would have to leave the island in the morning. He was a man of iron nerve and he answered "What has to be just has to be."

When morning came no smoke could be seen to the east and we assumed that the fire had been extinguished or had burnt itself out. We were then unaware that logcutters, who had been taken thence aboard a steamboat, had been fighting the blaze for three days. This revelation came later when the Abitibi Power and Paper Company management maintained that the Ontario Government should pay the costs.

Having been so informed, I, as the senior ranger, refused to sign the application, the while I explained that the Government wasn't responsible for fires that erupted on privately-owned territory. That ruling was upheld much to the indignation of the claimants.

I wasn't unduly concerned about such problems in that early dawn as I studied those white-capped waves that pounded against the island from the south and made canoeing against a head wind hazardous.

Large seagulls calmly floated on the crests, vanishing and then reappearing with picturesque regularity.

Four miles away Long Point was clearly visible and it was the objective we had to reach before we would find calmer water in the southern bay. Lumb, cool as Arctic ice, awaited my decision without uttering a murmur of dissent. Yet, it would be his life, more than mine, that would be placed at stake. Belatedly we made the discovery that the two packsacks and my razor had vanished.

Fortunately we had with us enough canvas to cover the canoe and for the first and only time in my life I spread it across the top of the craft and left only enough open space to accommodate us. During the first mile or so we bobbed up and down like corks but suddenly the winds began to fade and midway to the point there was hardly a ripple on the toned down surface. The rest of the journey was uneventful.

The loss of those packsacks and the razor, which I bought in 1910 in Haileybury for six dollars and which I still have 53 years later, impelled us to return to the island after the winds had subsided a week later. I discovered the razor under the balsam bed but the packsacks had been swept away and we could only suppose that they had disappeared into Davey Jones' locker.

With food supplies diminishing one week later we made the long trip to Lowbush and while we were there that evening a telegram was received in which it was stated that Foreman Billy Carmichael's daughter was seriously ill in Pembroke. We volunteered to cross that eleven miles of water on the errand of mercy although we knew it would be no sinecure.

When we emerged from the shadowy Lowbush river we found that the lake was in a raging fury. As far as the eye could see in that eerie moonlight glow we saw the leaping, white-capped waves thundering shoreward. "This is a three-quarter run", I yelled to Lumb, "We will go south-east and then south-west." He nodded in assent.

In those bounding waves the sturdy 16-foot Chestnut canoe dove and ascended, the while the howling winds shrieked past us. With the exception of the Mosher Mine island which didn't lie directly in our path there was no other sanctuary. Rough water never did appal me but as I watched Lumb I became the more convinced that he was the bravest of the brave, stoical and immune to fear. In me he had placed the greatest trust that a man can place in another.

Three and a half hours after we left the Lowbush river we stepped ashore at Hennessey's camp and delivered the message to Billy Carmichael. That day he was taken to Lowbush by motorboat and later we heard that his daughter had answered the 'last call'.

While en route back to the portage we visited a genius from Peterborough, an old man named McCarthy who sought to find perpetual motion. He lived on a high hill near where the Abitibi River begins and he was a friendly man who welcomed us with open arms.

In addition to furniture, which he had meticulously built without aid, he had erected a tall windmill with one of its purposes the drawing of water from a well which was 200 yards away and at water level. When he needed a pail of water he set the windmill in motion and during the operation that followed the pail would be lowered into the well and then to the cabin.

On the wall of the cabin there was a large grandfather's clock which, sans any winding, would produce the proper time through many months. But there was only one flaw that defied the achievement of perpetual motion and it was caused through wear and tear of the machinery involved.

McCarthy had a small rowboat to which he had attached a small windmill and sails that provided propulsion. He was a bit too canny, however, to take that contraption out in rough water and in explaining why, he said, "Only fools got out in canoes on Abitibi Lake and the worst fools who come this way are, if I may say so, those jackasses who are government rangers."

"Now, I had two of them up here several years ago and one was a preacher and the other was a nitwit from Manitoulin Island. The only time that nitwit exhibited any sense was when he wasn't sober. The sky pilot tried to reform him but always talked to him when he was sober. When he was 'tight', which was nearly every day, he tried to reform the preacher. Ah, wurra, wurra, I have never seed anything like it."

"Now just down river there is Couchiching Falls which is ninety feet high and every time I see that pair aboard a canoe in the river I get down on my knees and pray that they won't get caught in the current. Of course if they go over the Couchiching they will be knocking at the Pearly Gates immediately."

"And then below that there is the Island Rapids which no canoeist has ever run and lived to tell the tale. It is a very narrow strip of water and it looks innocent enough but it is rock-strewn and is as swift as lightning. About eight years ago, or was it longer, two damn fools from Mattawa went thirty-nine miles down the Abitibi and fifteen miles up the Black in eleven hours and fifty-six minutes but they didn't jump the Island, the Lower Couchiching or the two Twin Falls."

"By an odd coincidence", I replied "I come from Mattawa and I know the canoeists to whom you refer. They are Billy LeHeup and George Train and they are experienced paddlers. I heard long ago that they had established the record but I never knew the details."

"They were pretty smart', said McCarthy, "but that young 'un, Graham Hennessey from Haileybury, shoulda' had his head read. He tried to run one of those rapids or falls when the water was low but the canoe struck a rock and upset. Some say it was the Lower Twin after the dams had almost wiped it out. Damn near wiped him out, too."

"We'll be going to Matheson in a week or two," I said, "and I'll take a look at the storied Island Rapids."

"It won't do any harm to look at it", said McCarthy, "but use the portage and I'll be seeing you again."

An Indian named Fox and his heavyweight daughter lived directly across the river from McCarthy's abode and, in rare good fun, I assured him that I had never seen such a beautiful girl. The old chief replied "She ain't good lookin' but she is a good cook."

"Well, if she is," I retorted, "she should come over to the portage and she can bake some bread. My partner, who is studying to be a doctor, says that if he has to eat any more bannock he will collapse." Fox said nothing in reply but three days later he and the daughter, who had brought along all her clothes, arrived at our camp.

I was away fishing on the portage lake when the pair walked in and caught Lumb by surprise. The following conversation ensued...

Fox – "Here she is and she can stay all summer at five dollars a month."

Lumb – (Who hadn't heard about my jesting plea in his behalf) "She can't stay here and we don't need a cook."

Fox – "Do you think I paddle six mile for nothing? She's goin' to stay."

Lumb – "But she can't stay here. There is only one room and two beds."

Fox – "Lizzie she sleep on the blankette on the floor."

Lumb – "You don't say. Take her back home and if we need her we'll send for her."

At that moment I arrived and blandly inquired, "What is going on here?"

Lumb – "You tell me"...

Fox – "You say, 'Bring Lizzie here', and I bring. Now she stay or I shoot."

I replied, "Sure, I say 'bring' but it is only so that she can show Lumb how to bake the bread, not sleep in the bed."

Fox – "White man damn fools and you the biggest fool. Me leave. Take Lizzie, too and to h— with you."

153

Actually, I felt a bit guilty about the affair so I said, "Can Lizzie make raspberry vinegar? We have two pails of berries going to waste."

Fox - "She make the raspberry vinegar well. She also make wine from the dandelions. I betcha you see three mountains where there isn't any."

"Well," I said, "we have to go to the Narrows so she can make the vinegar but never mind the wine."

Three hours later when we checked in again Lizzie had all the jars in the shack loaded with steaming raspberry vinegar but we didn't sample it until the following evening. Lizzie, who, with her father, had departed, had poured a bottle of vinegar into the raspberry juice and when Lumb tested it I feared that he would choke to death.

To make matters worse, Lizzie had used twelve quarts of berries which we had picked in that 'raspberry paradise'.

Directly in front of our camp there was a fabulous swimming beach which extended for many miles along the point and the main shore. In wading width it was approximately half a mile and there was no undertow. When storms were at their height and high waves came thundering in we waded or we swam in that amazingly warm water.

On the east side of the portage similar conditions prevailed with the sole exception that the sandy bottom was strewn with deadheads. Thereof, one day when we had nothing else to do we decided to paddle around the point and return along the western shore.

It was a beautiful day when we began the fifteen mile trip but at the halfway mark when we were three miles from the mainland, the skies darkened and I turned due south to the western point. Suddenly, in the distance I saw, to my amazement, an oncoming waterspout that appeared to reach almost up to the clouds.

As nothing could be gained by warning Lumb, who hadn't seen it, I suggested that a sprint to the shore would provide excellent exercise. He responded and we drove onward at a very swift pace. Out of the corner of my right eye I saw that waterspout roll by and it was only then that I told Lumb what had occurred. But I doubt that he ever has believed that statement of fact. I can hardly believe it myself.

Strangely enough, the lake remained calm during the next several days before we left for Matheson to bring my brother Eddie to our camp for a holiday. It was our first trip down the first thirty-four miles of the Abitibi River and we avoided risks by using the three portages.

CHAPTER 17

Where Death Lurked

I took advantage of the opportunity to study the dreaded Island Rapids and I reached the conclusion that it must be conquered. It was probably fifty feet wide but through that narrow gorge the waters of the expansive river raced at terrific speed. I realized then why McCarthy had spoken in such awe about the torrent wherein the Indians believed ghosts of the past bellowed in rage and defiance.

I did not mention to Lumb or to any one else that Indian tradition did not appal me but, secretly, I harbored the ambition to 'shoot the gap' at the next opportunity. We reached Matheson and returned without incident but futurities that would be forever memorable lay just ahead.

Eddie was an excellent swimmer but I warned him to remain aloof from the portage lake which gave me a creepy feeling of insecurity.

Eddie, however, was only thirteen years of age and he just didn't believe my stories about bears and their preference for the portage lake in hot weather.

One evening when I was out in the canoe alone Eddie departed for that inland lake and when on my return I was so informed by Lumb I hid in the gathering darkness near the trail and awaited his return. Eventually, I saw him in the gloaming and when he was directly opposite me I imitated, as best I could, the snarling of a bear, the while I trampled brush.

With electrifying speed – which he never again approached – Eddie left there in a cloud of dust, raced into the cottage and slammed and barred the door. In the rush he almost upset Lumb. I waited for about five minutes to let that lesson sink in and then, laughing heartily, I leisurely went back.

When Eddie discovered that he had been made the victim of a hoax he did not applaud such goings-on but thereafter he adhered to my advice that he mustn't do any wandering alone. As a matter of fact he employed better tact.

One morning we awakened to find that the Abitibi Company logging gang had erected two large tents on the shore that fronted our shack. They had come to clear Long Point of pulpwood and their presence made our fire ranging duties all the harder.

The foreman, whom I will call Larry Murphy, was a character in his own right and his Irish wit and rambling discourses were truly astonishing. He was in every sense of the word delightfully unique. When we approached the camp Murphy said. "Now, ye don't need to tell me that ye are Rangers. I could tell that with a blind eye. But I guess we'll have to put up with ye."

"I wouldn't know", I answered, "but you better keep a civil tongue under control or Lumb will throw your crew, one after the other or all together, into the lake. He is the strongest man in the history of Queen's

ANENT MICHAEL J.

and he'd toss you around like a bag of beans."

Murphy – "The h— ye say. Now, I seed stronger men on Lake Deschenes but I never seed anyone as strong as is Joe Lafranier although I have seed some who could make him look like thirty cents, which isn't likely. Now I could throw out ye– and Lumb, too– in a jiffy if I wasn't too busy which I ain't this foine morning."

At that stage the French-Canadian cook came out of the tent and he said, "Sapristi, eef you want some bean I geev you some before Murphy she get mad and clout de knockout."

Those beans, which had been baked in sand, were delicious and Joe Savard, the cook, didn't have to urge us to eat them. When we complimented him he said, "Eet is no wonder that you lak' de bean. I cook for Booth and, by gar, I get fired because the foreman she say the shantymen eet so much bean dat de company can't afford it."

"They are so good," I replied, "that they could tempt the men to steal some."

"Oh no," laughed Joe, "they don't stole nothin' from me. I got de shoot gun on the wall and it is loaded with salt and, by gar, eet is no fun to have de wounds in de salt."

I retorted, "I will bet you one 'dollaire' that some one will 'stole' the whole 'caboodle'."

"Eet is a bet," said Joe, "and I will guard la place."

That afternoon I called Joe down to the wharf to see a fish heart, attached only to the head, beating rhythmically in the water. I explained that reflex action caused that oddity and that a frog, minus its head, would retain movement of its limbs for a long time."

"Merci and sacre bleu", said Joe, "I am amaze."

A half hour later he was even more amazed when he discovered that a large pot of beans, six pounds of butter, a pail of marmalade, two dozen eggs and a large slab of bacon had vanished from the tent. "By gar," he said," de bear she's come for sure."

"I have reason to suspect," I replied, "that the bear was Eddie in disguise. You have lost the bet and you will never be a millionaire unless you protect de dollaire."

"Well," said Joe, "she was de beeg joke but you fool me because you mak' Heddie took de supplies when I'm looking at de fish. But I fool you, too, because de shoot gun is not loaded and de trigger is breaked. And anyway, Heddie is too young to be shooted."

As I handed back the 'dollaire' I said, "Keep a closer watch on those beans and don't forget that Lumb is thrifty and goes to Queen's."

Those sawyers and axemen were experts and in quick time they had cleared adjacent forests of pulpwood. The loggers assembled the same into booms and these were towed to the Abitibi River by motorboat with John Munro at the controls. Munro then returned and brought along a large pointer in which the workmen would be taken to headquarters.

Having been associated with Munro on the Black and Abitibi rivers, I approached him and said, "John, a storm is brewing in the west and I think it would be highly dangerous to take those men across." "The h— you say," said John, "I never have seen a storm this motorboat can't run."

I replied, "You are due to absorb a painful surprise when you strike that open water that is not protected by the point."

"Are you telling me?" he asked, scornfully. "Perhaps you should do the steering."

"I'll do just that", I said, "because Lumb and I have to get some supplies at the main camp."

Before departing with Eddie also aboard and the canoe trailing behind, I told the workmen, most of whom were Italians, that I anticipated rough going but that they must not panic. They were stoically unafraid. There were twenty-eight in the party.

The first windy blasts struck about a mile and a half out and I remarked to Murphy that those high rolling waves hurtling from the west would bounce that pointer around like they would a feather or a cork.

"Well, arragh and begorrah," said the double-talking Murphy, "I have never seed a storm that I was afraid of, not even on Lake Deschenes which is the roughest lake I ever seed except this one which isn't as rough. Now, you can have Abitibi because I don't want it."

Eddie, thoroughly enjoying the fun, ventured the opinion that he would prefer to be some place else. Munro, stoical and stern, remarked that the situation wasn't humorous. I said nothing but I knew that in another few minutes we would strike the storm in all its raging fury.

Three quarters of a mile away to our left there was a beach laden with stumps and deadheads and it was to that doubtful haven I planned to turn if I found that the men were in dire peril. In the howling wind the waves became so mountainous high that they lifted the prow of the pointer fifteen feet into the air. Then the straining towing rope would pull it down again, the while spray and water assailed the frantic passengers.

"Gawdam", roared Murphy. "This is the worst storm I have ever seed but Lake Deschenes is rougher by far although it never was as bad as this. Cut the rope and let them drift. No, don't cut the rope or we'll drift too, which isn't likely. Gawdam you Munro, stop your swearin'."

Eddie, undaunted, says, "Those Italians are getting quite a ride. They are on the roller-boller coaster and they are swearing like mad. No, some of them are praying and that's a good idea."

"Prayin'", said Murphy, "won't do them no good if that rope breaks. I have never seed anything like it but ye should see the bay of Fundy which is worse but it can't possibly be. Gawdam it, I've been prayin' since we hit this storm over yonder."

In the distance I saw that the storm was increasing in violence so I swung the boat directly south and took it to low water in the bay where we found temporary refuge behind a small isle. "Gawdam," said Murphy, "you are the greatest steersman I have ever seed but I've seed a lot of others who had a lot more sense."

"Shut up", said Munro, "or I'll throw you overboard."

"Throw me overboard", replied Murphy," why, I never have seed a Scotchman who could throw anybody overboard except that I seen lots of them who could throw us all overboard. Gawdam it, don't go near that pointer or the Eyetalians will throw us in the drink, which isn't likely."

Stead Lumb, who had been watching that frightening panorama in silence, the while he had exhibited little concern, asked, "Where do we go from here?"

"Why, we're going right through." I answered, "along the south shore, past that island in the river and to the landing wharf."

In a few minutes we reached the river and in front of his cottage we could see McCarthy wildly waving his arms and pointing to the sky. He had been watching us since we left the portage and he knew, as he said later, that, "Only damn fool fire rangers would thumb their noses at Abitibi Lake."

One week after that perilous trip we locked the shack and left for Matheson sixty miles away. We stopped for a few minutes at McCarthy's landing and when he came down to meet us I told him we were going to try to crack the record and that we would run the Lower Couchiching and the Lower Twin. "And may God have mercy on your souls", he replied.

CHAPTER 18

Once in a Lifetime

The river was exceptionally fast that memorable day when I became the only canoeist who ever ran the Island Rapids and lived to write about it. I hadn't exactly planned it that way and I didn't mention the idea to either Lumb or Eddie. My decision was reached on the spur of the moment, while Lumb and Eddie were carrying packsacks across the portage.

I remember that I studied the onrushing stream and discovered a winding route that might be navigable. Alone with my thoughts, I hesitated momentarily and then I cast the die that would court fame or, perhaps, death. As I approached the crest I held my breath in suspense because directly in my path a water-soaked log moved up and down under the surface.

That log was devoid of bark and I could see – but only in a flash – that parts of tree limbs were still attached to the trunk. They were sharp at the ends and one of them could quickly tear a hole in a canvas canoe. I paddled backwards when the log arose and then shot forward when it went down.

The canoe sped on as I steered it into the foam that adjoined the rocks because where there is white water there is generally sufficient depth. As the canoe streaked ahead I glimpsed just in front of me the dreaded eddy and cellar that had made the rapids unconquerable, had claimed lives and would claim more.

I went to the outside adjacent to the inviting but dangerous backwater and as the canoe quivered I silently mumbled "No, not now." Through that narrow channel, which was about two feet wide, the streaking canoe leaped the gap and the gamble was over.

Owing to the pulling and upsetting power of the innocent-looking backwater, which is a scourge to canoeists, I went down river about a quarter of a mile before I turned the craft and coasted back to the lower wharf, there to find Lumb and Eddie almost on the verge of nervous collapse.

Gazing at me sternly, Lumb asked, "What kind of an inane idea was that?"

I answered, "I saved you the trouble of portaging the canoe."

"You did", said Lumb," but you risked your life and if you had been drowned Eddie and I would have been left stranded here forty-five miles by river from Matheson and much longer than that by trail."

"Forget it", I replied, "and if you behave yourself I'll take you and Eddie over the Lower Couchiching."

Just as we were ready to depart a French cook called Joe Simard came out of the woods and invited us to have a 'snack of bean'. He was a jolly fellow and, thereof, our visit became so memorable that even to this day Eddie vividly recalls his comical remarks which were somewhat as follows:

"I am not a cook; I am a chef" he orated, while winking an eye with speed, "I cook de bean and de breath and I mak' de baycone lak' nobody couldn't in de Toronto King Edward hotel. Now don't tak' only de one bean; tak' de pot."

"Thank you", said Eddie, as he picked up the pot and started for the door. "No, no", cried Joe, "I don't mean to tak' de pot complete. I mean tak' de bean what is in de pot."

Following that repast, Joe said; "You know someting. There's nobody ever run de Island Rapiddes. It is what you say, impos-sib-le. As for me, I stay on de shore and you nevaire get drown dat way; eh what."

"Perhaps no man in his sober senses ever ran the Island Rapids," retorted Lumb, "but you are looking at one right there who has just leaped the cataract."

"Mon Dieu", cried Joe, "you don't look lak that kind of a damn fool. What for you run de Island? Tole me dat. She's not suppose to be run, gawdam. Now, eef you're going to run dat rapiddes again tole me first and I will get de body down de riviere."

I didn't tell Joe that we were going to leap the Lower Couchiching but we did just that a short time later. It was a thrilling drop and ride but it lasted just a few seconds.

Moments later Lumb, confronted by spray and rock, suddenly pulled the canoe to the left and into the backwater. In a flash the craft swung to the left and turned due east. Fortunately, however, I had anticipated that such a mishap might occur and I kept the canoe upright by using the flat paddle method. In all fairness it should be said that my fine and willing partner had had little experience in rapids and fast water.

We portaged past the Upper Twin Falls but ran the Lower which had been reduced in height from about twenty feet to two. The current, however, swept the canoe against logs jammed on rocks and it almost upset. I might say at this time that I have paddled thousands of miles in all kinds of water and have never been upset.

The river was vastly higher than I had ever known it to be before but it didn't slacken our speed. With the time spent for dinner at Joe's camp deducted we completed that thirty-nine mile Abitibi river run in a breath-taking four hours and twenty-eight minutes; far ahead of the anticipated time schedule.

But we absorbed a shock when we turned into the Black where as far as we could see the stream was jammed with logs. "Well," said Lumb, laconically, "this is the end of the road to a record."

"You could be right", I replied, "but we'll hit the old bush trail that is submerged in water but appears to be barren of logs."

During the next five miles we followed that winding route, at a swift pace before we returned to the river proper not too far distant below the abandoned Abitibi Pulp and Paper Company gravel pit. We still had ten miles to go but all was smooth 'sailing' thereafter and we reached the Matheson dock in eight hours flat; three hours and 56 minutes ahead of the old record.

Eddie caught the first southbound train and the next day Lumb and I made the long trek back to Abitibi Lake. We started at daylight and the evening sun was fading fast when we reached McCarthy's landing. We remained overnight at Hennessey's camp and arrived at the portage the following morning.

When the news spread that I had run the Island Rapids debates became rampant in the logging camps with majority opinion insisting that it was all a hoax. McCarthy, as a recognized expert, was interviewed and I was told later that he orated somewhat as follows:

"No man with the semblance of a brain in his head would attempt to leap the cataract but Rodden is a fire ranger and most fire rangers I have seen just haven't got much sense. Of course, there are exceptions like Lumb. Now, there is a man after me own heart and he'll live a long time if he stays on the shore."

Most unfortunately, it must be told that Superintendent John Hennessey and Foreman Joe Lafranier of the Abitibi Power and Paper Company later lost their lives when they either tried to run, or were swept into the snarling Island Rapids. Their bodies were discovered deep in the forest after flood waters had receded the following spring.

I prefer to believe, although nobody knows, that they ventured too close to the rapids and then could not escape. The water above the Island runs at a rapid rate adjacent to the north shore but when I was there a protective boom had been strung across the river.

Personally, I never would have challenged the Island Rapids with a companion in the canoe. Moreover, Hennessey and Lafranier were heavyweights who would have reduced canoe clearance above water to a dangerous four inches or less. Canoes so loaded sink below the safety level and strike deadheads or hidden rocks.

Mr. Hennessey was a gruff-talking man but he had never raised his voice in anger when speaking to me. Lafranier, serious, capable and kindly, was admired by those he commanded. Somehow, I can't believe that he would have willingly challenged the Island scourge but if Hennessey gave that order he would not have backed away. "God rest them merry, gentlemen," is my tribute to them.

When news trickled through that the 'First Great War' had begun I was anxious to enlist and I so informed Stead Lumb. "Your life is your own," he replied, "but if you cast that die the road ahead will be perilous. This won't be any skirmish. Make no mistake about that." He spoke no idle words.

I thought the matter over for several days and then decided that I would go to Haileybury and join the Algonquin Rifles who later were aligned with the 48th Highlanders of Toronto. Having said farewell to Lumb, I crossed Abitibi Lake to Lowbush in a company boat; travelled to Cochrane on a motor-driven hand-car and arrived in Haileybury the next day.

My mother, quite naturally, was worried and she opposed that quick leap into Armageddon. My father, shrewd and reserved, did not portray his convictions. Thereof, I notified Captain Ferguson, a Mattawan, that I desired to join the Rifles where I would be with friends.

I never discovered what occurred behind the scenes but I vividly recall that Captain Ferguson met me on the main street and said; "we won't be taking you along and, say, aren't you employed by the Ontario Government?" When I answered in the affirmative he said something to the effect that I should keep the home fires burning before I got badly burned myself.

I resented that verdict but there was nothing I could do about it. I, however, went to the T & NO station to say goodbye to those brave pals, many of whom did not return from those blood-stained fields in Europe. One of them named McIntyre, who didn't come back, took a pet squirrel with him as his lucky charm.

In regret and disgust, I went north again and rejoined Lumb who had been all alone at the portage. He was glad to see me but he kept his own counsel and did not assail me with questions. Oddly enough, I enlisted twice after that rejection but circumstances over which I had had no control kept me aloof from the armed forces.

With September approaching I suggested that at break-up time we should travel by canoe and portage from Abitibi to Lake Temiskaming and try to find gold along the route that would take us through terrain where the Noranda and other mines now stand. Stead, however, could not afford the time because he was due to return to the Queen's University Medical course late that month. He would also be aligned with the Tricolor senior football team.

I had worn Queen's regalia in hockey and football during four campaigns but owing to the fact that I had been unfairly beaten in the election for the captaincy I had decided to join the McGill University Redmen who were under the coaching guidance of the famous Frank

Shaughnessy. Lumb understood perfectly the reasons why.

Midway through that summer I had received a letter from the late Professor Lindsay Malcolm, the Gaels' new mentor, in which he assured me that I would be re-admitted to the Medical course. I had lost my first year as a budding doctor but I knew that I had actually failed only in the anatomy examination.

Of interest is the fact that two years later, when I was employed in Kingston by the Canadian Locomotive Company in the shell-making department, I rented a house which was owned by one of my former teachers. There in the cellar one evening I found examination papers and, being curious, I examined them.

On the paper I had written the professor had originally awarded me 74 marks, 14 above the passing total of 60. Later, no doubt, he had drawn a large zero over an answer that was correct and had been allotted 15 points. By subtracting 15 from 74 he made it 59, one below the passing mark.

Four other students, who later became doctors, had failed in that test but officially all had passed. They were all friends of mine and they had written those examinations in close proximity to my desk. I wasn't too astonished when I made those discoveries but it was too late then to claim redress.

In reply to Lindsay Malcolm's letter sent to me at Abitibi Lake I briefly wrote; "I'll be seeing you in the fall, without a doubt, but I'll be wearing the Red and White of Old McGill."

I frankly admit that I wasn't a good student. I just couldn't decide what profession I wished to follow. In football I had been plagued with injuries, sustained mainly because of inferior equipment. By choice I had been a middle wing, now known as tackle, and at 158 pounds I was then the lightest by far in the Intercollegiate Union.

Inclusive of the seasons 1910, '11, '12 and '13 I had, in addition to middle wing, played at centre, outside wing, flying wing, quarterback and halfback and I had been awarded All-Star rating in no less than four of those berths. It is a record never equalled in the long history of Canadian football. But now I run alone in reliving such memories which are still a verdant green.

One evening as we sat near a camp fire I asked Stead Lumb what he planned to do. He replied, "I'll play football again and eventually I hope that I will be a doctor. And then who knows? Much depends on the duration of the war but, as of now, I do not visualize my participation in the same. But, I wouldn't know."

Fate provides such answers and Stead Lumb eventually marched away to war as a member of the Medical Corps. He saw a lot of action and I believe he was at the Dardenelles when British warships tried to run the straits. He was also at Soloniki and those he has since served so well in the vicinity of Bancroft, Ontario, revere him.

I have never had a better friend than Stead Lumb. He has toiled in the right and he has not failed. His courage and his confidence in my canoeing ability I will always treasure down that long trail that leads to Rainbow's End.

Following my return to Abitibi Lake, Lumb and I made only one more two-way crossing but we found plenty of excitement. During a visit to an abandoned mine we learned that the company had left behind a quantity of dynamite. We garnered a few sticks and used them in sinking a small shaft on a vein not far from the Forks river. If there was any gold there it was lifted high and far away in the blasting. Indian lore had it that there were huge white fish in the Narrows where the water was very deep so we dropped six sticks of dynamite into that channel but not a fish came up.

Unquestionably, there were numerous fish in the lake but that sand-strewn water probably prevented them from seeing trolls or bait. On a very hot day many miles from shore a huge muskie sank his teeth into the blade of my paddle but did not loiter around after he had gnashed that hard wood. We, however, saw him plainly just as he surfaced.

We found another muskie near the northern shore that was more than five feet in length. He had, however, perished through accident or old age and the aroma was such that we hastened into a head wind.

Raspberries, which grew in abundance, withered and died on the stems. Blueberries were even more numerous and they were large and sweet. There was one small island about a mile from the southern shore that, from a distance, looked like a vast blue ball. We tested its productiveness and we each filled a twelve-quart pail in approximately twenty minutes. Those berries grew in such clusters that they could be picked a handful at a time.

During a violent storm that was whipped up suddenly the only available sanctuary was a rock-bound shore against which the high waves struck and recoiled in seeming rage. As we moved along I detected a sandy opening and I said to Lumb;

"I will take the canoe in on the crest of a high wave where you can leap ashore and hold it until the next wave strikes. Then pull the canoe in quickly and ground it." After we both had landed safely Lumb quizzically asked, "And what is new?"

August passed and September arrived with its whispers of oncoming cold weather. At night we kept the stove burning and for amusement under lantern lights we played poker for chips alone, Black Jack and euchre. Then with the howling winds lathering the lake and swaying the trees we would find rest in slumber.

Life got a bit monotonous and we eagerly awaited that day in mid-September when we would make the last trip to Matheson. The trees were a sea of variegated colors and scenic beauty was everywhere. A week before we left, Eddie Gilligan of Mattawa came over the portage but he didn't recognize me, the reason being that I hadn't shaved for ten days and I sported something akin to red whiskers and a beard.

Gilligan was one of the best natural athletes I have ever known and he knew forests like he did the back of his hand. Unaware of my identity, he told us that he had found gold "away to the east and north of the lake" but that he had lost the trail and had been trying for two weeks to find the road back to the lake. He had also lost the claims he had staked.

When I realized that he didn't recognize me I said, "Judging by the way you carried that canoe I would venture the opinion that you come from Mattawa or Bonfield."

He answered "You have judged correctly but you don't look like a Sherlock Holmes. How on earth you reached that conclusion that I come from Mattawa is a mystery to me."

I replied; "You should know me. I used to play third base for the Mattawa Separate School team when you were the pitcher. You nearly ruined my hands when you hurled that ball to me with blinding speed."

"Now", said Gilligan, "I recognize you. And I also recall the day that you hurled the ball back at me with such speed that it went past me and knocked the hard hat off the principal's head."

"Yes," I replied, "and when the principal chased me I lost no time in making my first 'home run'."

As Gilligan paddled away to the Abitibi River I said to Lumb, "There goes one of the most daring and versatile men I have ever known. He holds one record that I don't think anybody else will ever match. When he was sixteen years of age he dove from the top of the 'Big White Bridge' across the Ottawa river near Mattawa and into the swift water ninety feet below. He resurfaced about 200 feet east of the bridge where the water runs swiftly en route to Johnston's Rapids where certain death awaited him but Gilligan swam out of the eddies and reached the Quebec shore."

"You Mattawans", laughed Lumb, "are fabulously foolish. Train and LeHoup run the Abitibi River and you go them one better by risking your life in defying the Island Rapids, the while your brother and I are faced with the propect of getting hopelessly lost when en route to Matheson."

"And did you ever hear of Gilligan's Rock?", I inquired.

"No," said Lumb, "but having nothing else to do I might as well listen in patience."

"Gilligan's Rock," I answered," is situated at the foot of the Ontario Laurentians on the Ottawa river about three miles north of Mattawa. On one side there is a precipice about sixty feet high and directly below, the rocks extend about twenty-five feet from shore."

"Following raids on hen coops, miscreants would attend bouillons on Gilligan's Rock, the while intoxicating drinks were served as a side line. Then when most of those night raiders could see only twinkling stars they would stage diving duels down into the darkness."

"All of which confirms my conviction," said Lumb, "that Mattawans should have their heads read."

"Have you" I asked, "ever heard the story...?"

"No," roared Lumb, with definite finality,"and I don't want to hear it."

Break-up time came in that lonely, eerie setting with a nip of frost, a bit of sleet and with the trees beginning to present a panorama of brilliant colors. In the dawn we loaded our belongings into the sturdy canoe that through all those months had served us so well on the wild waters of the unpredictable Abitibi.

The canoe hadn't escaped unscathed but holes in the canvas had been covered over with tar and gum. I bought it from the Government for a lowly $15 and took it to Haileybury where I used it one day in going to the rescue of a moose that had attracted many craft-born spectators after it had swum an estimated fifteen or more miles from the Quebec to the Ontario side of Lake Temiskaming. When that flotilla moved away the frightened and exhausted moose swam slowly to a small island, struggled ashore, staggered about twenty feet and dropped dead.

Our farewell to Abitibi Lake was memorable in that we never saw it again. We weren't in any hurry and thus we did not assail the record that we had established. We visited the recluse McCarthy briefly and he said. "If you aim to live let those Island Rapids roll on alone. To run that stretch once was the height of nonsense; to try it again would reek of sheer stupidity."

His advice was priceless and I assured him I would use the portage; which I did.

At Twin Falls we met some Abitibi Pulp and Paper Company employees who told us they were searching for the body of an unknown canoeist who had perished in that vicinity. As we moved down steam we scanned the swift river with negligible results. So we pushed on to Matheson and there, to my surprise, I learned that I was supposed to be the man who had a met a watery grave.

Just before we parted at Haileybury Lumb's wit impelled him to state that a very warm welcome would await me when the McGill Redmen went into football action against Queen's. "I'll be seeing you," I replied," and I wish you luck because I think you're going to need it."

(Note - In 1939 I was a fire ranger and game warden in Algonquin Park and three years later I filled the same dual role in the Shining Tree country)

CHAPTER 19
Hockey Days

While I was in Haileybury a report appeared in a Toronto newspaper that I had been drowned and in no time at all wreaths, flowers, telegrams and letters of sympathy cluttered my parent's home. The largest wreath was dispatched by the University of Toronto Athletic Directorate but Queen's ignored the matter.

My sister, a student at the University of Toronto, hastened home and, oddly enough, the first person she saw on the station platform was myself. I had gone to that depot to get my canoe.

I spent the 1914 football season with McGill until I was sidelined with a twisted ankle.

My departure from McGill brought to an end my university career which had started in 1906. I had previously spent slightly more than three academic years at the University of Ottawa and four at Queen's where I had met Millie Wormwith who later became my wife and will always be the sweetheart of my dreams.

From Toronto I returned to Haileybury where my brother Jack, manager of the arena and theatre, provided me with employment. Jack also organized the Temiskaming Hockey League which included the Cobalt Lake Mine, New Liskeard and Haileybury. It was an independent circuit and it was loaded with stars.

During that 1914-15 hockey season I played for Haileybury in the Temiskaming League and finished second as a point getter to the great Gordon "Duke" Keats in behalf of a machine that was composed of the following players: Goal - the late Bill Tobin, who many years later was aligned with the Chicago Black Hawks as business manager, manager or coach; defence - the late Fred Dennison of Peterborough, "Duke" Keats and myself; centre - brilliant Larry Lawrence of Collingwood; rover - Jerry Coughlin, a Peterborough ace, who later joined the Toronto NHL Arenas; left wing - Archie Briden, who was destined to see much professional service with Toronto Ontarios, Edmonton and the Boston Bruins; right wing - Ernie Fryer of Collingwood. Dinny Breen, a youthful alternate, eventually joined the Toronto St. Patrick's OHA seniors. Other alternates were 'Tee' Hillman and Sid Hooper.

During that series I played every position on the team, inclusive of goal when Bill Tobin was penalized in the Cobalt arena. On paper Haileybury had a powerful machine but the Cobalt Lake Miners were the class of the circuit. They captured the championship in a 2 game playoff series against Haileybury. During a long refereeing career in the NHL, I saw a lot of teams that would have been no match for those smooth-working Miners who were packed with stars and stressed cohesion.

Unquestionably, the following Cobalt Lake players were of major league status. Goal - Ray Bonney of Ottawa: defence - Jack Westlake, Port Arthur; and Mac McCarthy who later joined the Montreal

Canadiens; forwards - the late Mike Kennedy, University of Toronto; Bill Ross, a rover from Fort William who later was electrocuted in the Cobalt Lake Mine; Russ McCrimmen, a rightwinger and "Red" Fraser, a wingman whose terrific speed shooting has seldom been excelled by any other hockeyist. 'Brick' Brickendon was also a winger on the Miners.

New Liskeard, outclassed in the swift action, had only one player, Leo Reise, who eventually became a major leaguer. Keats, Briden and Coughlin, all of Haileybury, made the 'big time' grade and Keats, the greatest stickhandler in hockey history, is now a member of the Hall of Fame.

Those were bitterly-waged battles and there was one night in New Liskeard when Keats and I were so badly injured that we flirted with death. I was struck down via a butt-end on the temple delivered by the late Jack McLean and the injury was so serious that some misguided person informed a Toronto newspaper that I was dead. In the same game Keats almost lost an eye via a butt-end by McLean.

It was the third time that my untimely demise had been reported but as Mark Twain was wont to say, the facts had been greatly exaggerated. Actually, I played against New Liskeard several nights later and claimed a bit of a toll from big Jack McLean, who weighed a mere 242 pounds. McLean died in Toronto several years later allegedly as a result of injuries absorbed in hockey.

The Cobalt rink was an ice palace in more ways than one. It was a large barn-like structure that looked like an aeroplane hangar and therein had been waged some of the goriest games in history. But, strange as it may seem, the Haileybury team was more effective in that setting than it was on its own narrow ice surface.

There was one game there that none of the participants could ever forget. Outside the thermometer showed a 54 below zero Fahrenheit reading and inside it was a frosty minus 35. Owing to the release of the regular right winger I was assigned to that patrol and through a bit of good fortune I managed to score three goals.

Such goings-on caused a bit of disunity, so in that dire emergency and with Cobalt leading 4 to 3, I voluntarily left the game and sought the heat of the dressing room. Ten minutes later the Haileyburians trooped in and, with great disgust, reported they had been beaten 7 to 4.

Our next trip to Cobalt was memorable in that Haileybury scored the first four goals; Cobalt the next five and Haileybury the last two in a 6-5 victory. Larry Lawrence, who would have become a major leaguer if illness hadn't ended his career, racked up the deadlocking counter and I got the winner with less than a minute left in regulation time.

I was a rather fast skater but I was never a gifted hockeyist although I did reject two offers to become a National leaguer. Three years later I came out of retirement when the Toronto St. Patrick's OHA senior team needed help but at season's end I wrote 'finis' to my hockey career as a player.

In 1915 I accepted a position as a clerk in the Cochrane office of the Canadian National Railways; the salary being a staggering $55 per month out of which I had to pay all living expenses. $35 of that salary was spent for a room and meals in the Cedric hotel, leaving a total of $20 for clothes and other expenses. I was, however, told that at the end of the first year I could apply for an increase, which, if granted, I wouldn't receive before another six or twelve months had elapsed.

The lone bright lining in the clouds was the fact that "Roxy" Beaudro, former dazzling rover of the Rat Portage-Kenora Thistles, was the chief clerk. Beaudro, one of the fastest skating players in hockey history, taught me the time-keeping art and thereafter I was unofficially in charge of that department.

Strangely enough, some of the employees who, like myself, were a bit underpaid, held me responsible for the lowly stipends they received. One of them, a Scotsman whom I will call Marston, received the stupendous sum of $40 a month for acting as the freight agent.

When I handed him his first cheque he threw it on the office floor, stamped on it and then walked out.

I reported the matter to Beaudro who smiled and said, "This must be the first time a Scotsman ever scorned $40. I will place the cheque in the safe and I will wager that he will return to claim it tomorrow morning."

That evening when I was in conversation with two railroad employees in a restaurant Marston strolled in and called one in the party a foul name. As he wasn't looking at me I gained the impression that he was verbally assailing a brakeman named Doherty.

After Marston had departed I asked Doherty why he hadn't taken issue with such an allegation. "Why should I," he answered, "when he was insulting you?"

As we left the restaurant Marston confronted me on the board sidewalk and announced that he was about to hand me a thrashing that I would not soon forget. "A Scotsman," he said, "never surrenders." But he erred slightly and on arising from the mud-laden street he rushed to police headquarters and charged me with assault. When I appeared in court the next morning the procedure was somewhat as follows:

Magistrate Dempsey –"Hear ye all. What say ye Marston against the defendant?"

Marston – "He didna' whip me in a fair fight. He held ma head in the mud and he demanded that I surrender. But I wouldn' surrender so he pushed ma head doon again and I surrendered, ye ken."

Magistrate – "The defendant will now be heard. Did ye give this complainant a mud bath in the street?"

Rodden – "That I did but I did not request him to surrender. I did, however, demand that he must retract the foul statement that he had addressed to me."

Magistrate – "Why didn't you report the matter to me? This taking of the law into your own hands is most reprehensible."

Rodden - "I have heard that under somewhat similar circumstances last winter you knocked down a detractor in front of the Cedric hotel. Why didn't you appeal to the law?"

Magistrate - "I happen to represent the law in this town and how could I appeal to myself? Now; if you hadn't admitted your guilt I would dismiss the case. Of course, I am proud of you because you're a bit like your cousin Tom McGarry but I must fine you ten dollars and five extra for the trouble."

Lloyd Drinkwater (a friend of mine who had seen the eruption)– "With your permission, your lordship, I will pay the fine and costs. Michael is an innocent man but he punches with painful authority."

Magistrate - "The case is dismissed but I do commend the defendant for his frankness and honesty."

The second act occurred across the street in the Cedric hotel poolroom a few minutes later. In addition to the writer those in attendance were: "King" Dodds, who had found a bit of gold in the Kowkash river country 320 miles west of Cochrane, Lloyd Drinkwater, Joe Rothschild, Marston and Doherty.

"King" Dodds, who had attended the trial with $5,000 in his pockets, strolled over to Marston and scornfully said, "Are ye fully aware that your cowardice is not appreciated in this here mud belt? I will gladly pay ye, not the court, $15 for the privilege of knocking ye down."

"Nae, nae", roared Marston, "I weel hae none o' that."

But he spoke too late. Dodds knocked him down; threw $15 at him and strolled out into the cooler air.

Cochrane of that era had a cosmopolitan population reminiscent of the 'Wild West' and danger seemed to lurk around every corner. Trainmen and section hands, who had been dismissed by the CPR and the old Grand Trunk lines and who had been given employment by the CNR, were rather numerous and some of them hadn't completely reformed.

Those of us who worked in the head office were called stooges and white collar misfits. As the timekeeping clerk, I was regarded with grave suspicion and especially so when members of the freight crews did, in accordance with the mileage paying system, draw far larger stipends than did engineers, conductors and brakemen who were in passenger service.

One evening when I attempted to enter a restaurant a T & NO brakeman named Furlough barred the way and threatened to throw me into nearby Lake Commando. He was known as a tough hombre who was feared, if not respected. When I politely asked him to desist from such nonsense he sneeringly stated "no white collar misfit could remove him from the steps."

Lloyd Drinkwater, who was with me, warned the brakeman that he might be overmatching himself. Furlough's peals of laughter and his salty language attracted the attention of passersby who did not 'pass' too far. Then suddenly, Eddie Gilligan, of whom I have written before, emerged from the restaurant and surveyed the scene.

"Well, upon my word", said Gilligan, "I thought I recognized your voice. And who is this blatherskite who would deny you admittance to this eating establishment?"

"He appears to be", I replied, "the owner of the restaurant, the mayor the town and the acting police chief."

"Well, notwithstanding his importance to the community", said Gilligan, "I will wager that you will win the debate."

Mr. Furlough's reaction was lightning swift. Pointing to a yard behind the Queen's hotel he said, "That is where this argument will be settled."

And, thereof, we repaired to the yard where the great discovery was made that Furlough should have gone on 'furlough' after Gilligan had rendered that prophetic oration.

In August of that year Millie Wormwith, daughter of the owner of the Wormwith and Weber Piano Company of Kingston and I were secretly married in Cochrane, the while snow fell heavily outside and Northern Lights flashed in the sky. No greater love and trust hath any girl than this, that she should so courageously defy her family, her advisors and her friends and marry a man who had to borrow $50 to buy a ring and pay the marriage fee.

Millie, a B.A. graduate of Queen's University, arrived on one train and departed on the next, the while I was left to wonder if it had or hadn't been the most enchanting dream of my life. And now in the evening of our lives, as we look back, we would have had it no other way. "When Destiny beckoned she did not hem nor stall. She is in fact the grandest girl of them all."

CHAPTER 20

"King" Dodds and the Kowkash

With futurities of importance approaching, I fully realized that severance of relations with the CNR had become mandatory. Thereof, I handed in my resignation and joined a party of three others who would do the assessment work on the 'gold' property which "King" Dodds had discovered 24 miles north of the CNR and 320 west of Cochrane.

Snow was falling heavily when we left Cochrane aboard the caboose of a freight train with an engineer named Larry Downey at the throttle. On that new line the speed limit was, for safety's sake, set at 35 miles per hour but the freight was so long and heavy that swift progress was out of the question. The engineer had orders to move onto a siding near Fauquier Junction to allow the east-bound passenger express the right-of-way.

Eventually we reached that siding with not much time to spare. Conductor Bill Hancock and a brakeman named Billy Webb tapped the telegraph wire and learned that the express would be due at any moment. Hancock signalled the warning to Downey who was striving with might and main to get all those cars off the main line.

There were still a half a dozen blocking the line, when in the darkness, we saw the oncoming express with big Joe Haystone holding the throttle and driving far above the limit, in an effort to make up lost time. When a collision seemed imminent we retreated from the tracks and scrambled up a high bank.

With the freight train moving slowly in fits and starts and with wheels slipping on the upgrade it didn't appear possible that the main line would be cleared but Downey performed that feat and just in the nick of time. Not more than a foot or so clearance was left when the express flashed past and spread the switch of its own accord.

As we stood there trembling in awe we espied the observation car as it sped into the darkness, the while passengers, unaware of danger, calmly smoked cigars and read newspapers. They would probably never know that the onrushing express had so narrowly escaped almost certain destruction.

Another fleeting picture that will be forever green in my memory was that presented by Engineer Joe Haystone as he gazed seemingly without concern into the distance. He had, however, seen the danger ahead after the engine had rounded a curve but the train's momentum had been too great to even slow it down.

Early the next morning we reached the Kowkash station and found refuge in a stopping place which was crowded with prospectors. They were adventurers who followed gold trails with hope springing eternal that they would find an Eldorado. Men of that ilk would wager on anything and thus it came about that they organized a pool in which the money involved, $270, would be presented to the two canoeists who would reach the Dodds claim in first place.

Mr. Forbes, representing the Caldwell Company of Perth, which had paid $5,000 of a $150,000 option taken on the Dodds claim, aligned himself with the foreman and a dynamite expert named Pat Brogan in one canoe and willed unto me, as a partner, a large Dutchman who had never been in a canoe in his life.

To make matters even worse Mr. Forbes ordered the Dutchman and myself to await the arrival of the next train which would be carrying eatables and tools. That edict meant automatic withdrawal from the marathon and our entry fee was reclaimed. As I stood on the shore I counted the canoes and found that the total was twenty six. "Well", said the Dutchman, "those ahead of us will, at least, break the ice in the creek before they reach the fast-running Kowkash river."

Two hours after the first canoeists had left the dock we began the pursuit which seemed so hopeless. We passed seven in the three mile creek and twelve more during the first mile down the Kowkash. Straining at the paddles, we counted six other craft before we caught sight of the twenty-sixth as it neared a short portage adjacent to a falls that was considered unrunable.

At a glance I saw that we wouldn't reach the Dodds landing first if we had to use that portage. I had never seen the falls before but at the "steel" all had been warned that no canoe would survive a trip over the cataract and through the foaming rock-strewn rapids below it.

Quickly I suggested to the Dutchman that I would land him at the portage and then I would go over the falls and take along the load we carried. "If you go", replied the ice-cool Dutchman, "I go, too." Moments later we took the leap and it was a thrilling ride but as nothing in comparison to the running of the Island Rapids.

Three miles ahead of us the roaring Howard Falls, seventy feet in height and resembling a stairway, emptied into a rapids where the currents were tricky and fast. The portage began at its crest and we crossed it with speed. The rapids provided no problem and we reached Dodds landing far in advance of the closest pursuer. [Due to Forbes] we had lost $270 that we so direly needed.

Approximately two hours later the other company canoe hove into sight. We took up residence in a large log cabin and early the next morning began exploration work on the frozen ash-strewn ground where a fire had demolished most of the trees. Bits of gold glittered in the sun where the 'find' had been made but elsewhere all was barren desolation.

Mr. Forbes and his foreman decided then and there that they would blast out the discovery and sink a shaft below it. In no time at all the drills struck shale and proved that the claim had a hollow ring. Ignoring such signs Brogan daily blew out more of that shale until the shaft was ten feet in depth.

I searched the claim from end to end and also invaded the adjoining forest which stood in a swamp but gold was nowhere visible. Wearily, one night I reported to Mr. Forbes that we had embarked on the wildest goose chase of them all. But he persevered for three more weeks before he threw in the sponge.

A large moose shot out of season in the river provided excellent food but all of us who ate so ravenously became painfully ill. Daily we saw disgusted prospectors homeward bound and very few of them exhibited any interest in the Dodds claim.

One evening in the gloaming two prospectors came into our cabin and one of them was Pat McDonough of Haileybury. Tersely, he told me that if there was any gold in the Kowkash country it must have been deliberately planted. He also stated that he had found gold in another locality but that he was bound by agreement to keep the matter a secret.

That discovery I learned later – but too late – had been made on a veteran's lot in the Kirkland Lake district or at Boston Creek and negotiations for its sale had been opened with the owner who resided in England. Thereof, secrecy was demandatory because McDonough and his associates aimed to complete the deal before other prospectors could honeycomb that terrain. The rush came while I was en route to Haileybury several weeks later.

I made one canoe trip along to the Kowkash siding to get supplies and mail and during that journey I paddled up a falls that others wouldn't leap with the current. Much to the surprise of my companions, I returned the same day and reached the camp before sundown. The total distance covered was forty-eight miles.

Although we found little gold, there were stories told that rate repetition. "King" Dodds, a wayfarer from Toronto, had severed family ties and through many years had lived in the wilderness with Indians being his only associates.

One Christmas Eve Dodds, the chief and two squaws did partake too much of intoxicants and the discussions became rather heated. The chief, convinced that Dodds aimed to marry one of his daughters, strongly objected and ordered Dodds to vacate the premises and reached for a rifle as a persuader.

Not desiring such a swift demise, Dodds hurled a whiskey bottle with such unerring aim that it struck the chief on the brow and knocked him colder than a mackerel. Presuming that he had passed into the land of his fathers, Dodds placed the chief aboard a toboggan and hid the 'remains' in the forest three miles away.

Dodds then returned to the teepee, sympathized with the mourners and soon fell fast asleep. Dawn was just breaking when the chief parted the drapes, staggered into the tent and with a thunderous roar awakened the occupants. "Dodds", he asked, "what are you doing here? Get out before I get too mad."

Dodds, suddenly remembering that it was Christmas Day, lost no time at all in sprinting homeward. Later, however, he participated in another misunderstanding that had comical after effects. Through no fault of his own, a young squaw in the vicinity toiled under the impression that he would marry her. The 'King' had other ideas and took refuge near Sullivan Lake, a noted fishing locale.

There one day an Indian courier found him and presented him with the following letter from his admirer Annie Fireflower.

"Dere King; Why did you leave me in the perch? I love you very much so please come back. But you are no good and I wouldn't marry you, no sir, not me. Joe Antoine he give me the ring but I give it back because I marry just you who are no good.

"I think of you all the time but why I don't know why unless it is because I am the fool. But if you come back, which I hope you won't, we could get married and go out and catch the beaver. Well, anyway, the h—- with you and if you don't marry me I will shoot you first time I see you which I hope will be soon. Your lovin' Annie."

The 'King' wasn't greatly impressed but he did laughingly show me the above letter, the while he sighed, "I'm damned if I know what ails that beautiful lady."

One very cold morning I ventured out to get wood for the stove and there before my startled eyes I saw a jet black fox of a species so rare that its fur would have brought a fabulous price. Momentarily, he stood on his hind feet near a fallen tree and then, like a flash, he was gone. I followed his tracks for a half mile or so and found that he had vanished in swampy land.

When the shaft on that mysterious discovery was fourteen feet deep I advised Mr. Forbes that to blast any more would place Brogan in great peril. There had been occasions when it was feared that Brogan might not escape after he had ignited fuses attached to the dynamite. I had had experience in Cobalt mines and I had never seen a trap worse than that on the Dodds claim.

Owing to the shale and the distances it and rocks travelled following the explosions, we had built a protective log wall about 200 yards from the shaft and behind that we crouched in the interests of safety.

Eventually, Mr. Forbes tossed in the sponge and announced that they would start the trip to the 'steel' (the railroad) the following morning. He also stated that the foreman, Brogan and the Dutchman would man one canoe and that he would be aligned with me in the other.

We were the first to get away and after ascending the rapids we awaited the arrival of the other canoe, the while I ventured the opinion that the two aboard would experience great trouble in that fast-running current.

When we espied them I was astonished to see that Brogan, wearing a very wide-brimmed hat, was sitting high on a packsack in the middle of the bobbing craft. There were two routes, one on the west shore and the other on the east, that the foreman should have followed but, lo and behold, he tried to climb through the rock-bound centre where the current was at its swiftest.

Just as they reached the halfway mark the canoe suddenly spun around and Brogan was cast into the stream, the while the wind blew his hat into the distance. Brogan grasped a rock about six inches below the surface and stood on it but not with the grace of a tight rope walker. The canoe, unmanageable, drifted to the west shore.

Without any waste of time I ran the rapids and rescued Brogan, whose teeth were chattering from the cold. I paddled to the east shore, allotted him a bow berth and proceeded to the portage. The foreman and the Dutchman followed in our wake and landed without further incident.

About six miles farther up the river Mr. Forbes investigated another property and appeared to be in no hurry at all. In the hope that I might collect a few fish I paddled into a low creek but saw very few of any species. Previously on a Sunday afternoon I had gone up a narrow creek near the Dodds claim and therein I had seen large and small fish packed so densely that they could be caught by hand. I had taken a muskie, several beautiful trout and three black bass back to camp.

Sullivan lake, into which the waters of the Kowkash flow, was alleged to be the most productive fishing centre in that vast and lonely area. Only a few Indians lived in that vicinity and under such circumstances fish multiplied by the thousands.

Several groups of prospectors who had gone that far north – about seventy miles from the railroad – had attempted to regain money expended by shipping a carload of fish to Toronto but all those members of the finny tribe had been lost in a train wreck. The car carrying the fish had tumbled down a steep bank and the 'fish story' ended right there.

When Mr. Forbes returned it was almost three o'clock and we had eighteen miles to go; fifteen of them against the stiffening current. In another hour or so the river would be blotted out in darkness. Progress would be retarded because Forbes, as the bowman, could paddle only on his left side. Moreover, he was no expert in a frail canoe.

Three and a half hours later we reached the narrow creek which was partly frozen over, was weedy and strewn with deadheads, small islets and rocks. Thus, in the interests of safety, the slow approach became mandatory. In the bitter cold our hands neared the freezing point.

Finally, with about a mile to go I espied just ahead of us a moving object and a few minutes later as we drew alongside we saw Brogan, the foreman and the Dutchman.

"Gawdam", said the Dutchman, "we have been all over the river and the creek. I don't know how to steer, the boss is worse and Brogan is a passenger. Is there any end to this damn creek?"

"Follow me, "I answered, "and you'll be at the steel in another fifteen minutes." "Merciful God", chattered the Dutchman, "if you hadn't arrived we would have been out here all night."

At the dock we unloaded our belongings and carried them to an adjacent stopping place where the owner quizzically inquired, "Did you see any others on the river? I would wager that you didn't because according to my count you are the last of the damn fools who tried to find gold in this God-forsaken country."

"We did find a bit of gold on the Dodds claim," said Forbes, "but under that discovery there was nothing but shale."

The proprietor, laughing heartily, said; "Those experts from Winnipeg who travelled by special car swore that if there is any gold in this here country it was planted. They spent thousands of dollars and they found nothing."

"If Dodds", I answered, "had planted that gold he wouldn't have invited exposure of the fraud by burning down the trees on the claim. It was owing to that act that we learned there was no gold anywhere, other than at the point of discovery."

"Well, some of them made money," he answered, "and of course, others didn't during poker games played in this cabin. And I didn't do badly but I hear there will be a rush on Boston Creek so you better get there fast. Some fellow from Haileybury named McDonough found the shining metal there on a veteran's claim."

On arrival in Cochrane I went to the Cedric hotel in pursuit of my trunk, in which my best suit of clothes reposed, but the owner informed me that he was holding it until I paid the balance allegedly owing for board and room at $50 a month. I retorted, "I owe you nothing. The arrangement was that I would pay $35 a month."

Maintaining that he knew nothing about such an agreement, Mr. Rothschild refused to release the trunk but he was courting a surprise. Two days later I reported the matter to Arthur Slaght, one of Canada's most brilliant lawyers, whose head office was in Haileybury. Mr. Slaght acted quickly and the trunk reached Haileybury the following day.

Torn between conflicting emotions and beset by problems, I returned to the LaRose Mine as a machine helper under the command of Captain Leonard Fyfe. The mine was being operated with a reduced staff of workmen and quite soon I became engaged in various tasks. It was back-breaking toil and the stipends were small.

Following a near-fatal accident, which involved five miners and myself, all underground employees were informed that they must descend to and come up from the levels via ladders and not by the hoisting cage. The lowest level – or tunnel – was 200 feet down and the edict that closed the cage route was resented by the miners.

CHAPTER 21

Moment of Decision

Christmas passed and in January I applied for admittance to the Queen's University Second Division Engineers who were in training in Kingston for overseas duty. My application was accepted and a railroad passenger ticket was dispatched to me. I then notified my wife about the matter and, with no other choice to make, she told her parents that we were married. She sent me a telegram to that effect and the great moment of decision had arrived.

In full realization that I could not provide my wife with life's necessities at a private's salary of a dollar and ten cents a day, I borrowed $50 from John McMahon, went to Kingston at my own expense and secured employment making shells in the Canadian Locomotive Company works. My wife and I rented two rooms and ate at a boarding house.

Shortly thereafter I was officially informed that I must report for duty with the Engineers, all of whom I knew quite well. So I reported but not in the manner expected. Ralph Hagey, the commanding officer, had been one of my teammates on Queen's senior football teams and he knew about the problems that confronted me.

When I walked into the room he said "Salute" and I icily replied, "Salute whom?" I then explained that if he could make arrangements whereby I would be granted a commission, I would go overseas in world's record time. Unable to meet that demand, he told me that I was free to do as I pleased.

My original pay at the CLC was 20¢ an hour or two dollars a day; the total being $11 a week; only $3.30 more than I would have received as an Engineer. I need hardly stress the fact that we had to adhere so closely to a small financial budget that luxuries were out of bounds.

I was a helper on a waving machine during the first three weeks and then was placed in charge of one. The highest output per day had been eight, and that not frequently. I soon raised that via the piece work plan until my daily stipends ranged between $10 and $15.

But conditions were a bit chaotic and the two foremen in charge did not seem to appreciate such donations to the cause. Machine men doing the waving and applying the copper bands assembled more coin of the realm than did the said foremen.

I will not relate in detail the episodes that occurred but some of them rate mention. Owing to a monumental blunder made by inspectors, hundreds of shells had been passed although the waving machines hadn't achieved the proper depth, which was finely drawn to the ten thousandth part of an inch.

When that discovery was made I was ordered to provide that depth; a task so difficult that the six-a-day output would be restored. I suggested that qualified machinists should be assigned to the task. My refusal definitely did not increase my waning popularity with the men in charge.

During a lull in 1917, I acted as an inspector in the Wormwith and Weber Piano Factory which had been founded and later sold by my father-in-law. My salary was, however, below what I had been earning so I reverted to the CLC after that company had received a contract to manufacture smaller shells.

Those shells were easily waved but the management didn't 'wave' in applauding my take-home-pay. Thereof, when on the third successive morning I found that the cutters on the machine had been deliberately reduced to needle points I notified the superintendent and the two foremen that I had reached the end of the line.

The heavyweight foremen were in their glass-enclosed office and were in conversation with an English inspector named Hayes when I walked in. What I said to them can readily be imagined. I charged them with being envious because I was making more money than they were being paid.

Bitter words were exchanged and the larger of the foremen stated that he would like to meet me outside the plant. When I assured him I'd be there the inspector stated that he would welcome the opportunity to 'box' my ears. Beside him there was a large waste paper basket into which I tossed him headlong. I then left the plant.

That evening I went to the large foreman's home on Montreal Street and invited him to discuss matters outside. But he elected to remain 'inside'. The next day Mr. Farr, the superintendent, appealed to me to return but I declined. He was concerned about output and he guessed correctly because following near-completion of that contract the CLC didn't get another one.

Notwithstanding arduous toil in 1916 when I worked the night shift, I had played for the Queen's University seniors in the Military Football League and had coached the Kingston CI juniors, who captured the eastern Ontario title by drubbing the Brockville CI gridmen on their own field 68 to 0.

That KCI machine was one of the greatest down memory's lane. It was sparked by John "Red" McKelvey, a halfback who was then just fifteen years of age. Others in the squad who later wore Queen's regalia were Fred Veale, "Pres" McLeod, Bill Campbell and the late "Foghorn" Dolan. My brother, Eddie, was the substitute quarterback.

Our first of two sons, William Bernard, was born on January 11th, 1917 and with living costs high it was imperative that I should receive steady employment. Thereof, I applied for wave-cutting duty to Tom Yellowley, a Kingstonian who had left the CLC to become superintendent of shell-making in the Russell Works plant in Toronto.

The Russell Company was turning out 300-pound shells and in accordance with a signed contract, had to deliver them on or before a specified date. However, a bottleneck occurred when machinists who were waving ridges for copper bands fell far behind schedule. Strange as it may seem, qualified machinists had also encountered similar setbacks in the CLC.

Mr. Yellowley lost no time in accepting my application and the die was cast that would lead to memorable experiences. On arrival in Toronto I found that conditions had not been exaggerated. Shells were piled high near the six waving machines and the total daily output, the night shift included, hovered around sixty.

Almost immediately I discovered that the revolving belts did not generate the proper speed and I so notified the man in charge. A machinist by trade, he was a tall, powerful man who tolerated no dictation and his salty remarks wooed neither tolerance nor admiration. He hailed from Shelburne, Ontario.

I reported the matter to Bill Sharpe, a brilliant machinist from Kingston who was Tom Yellowley's top aide. Mr. Sharpe responded by ordering the demanded alteration and the machines began to sing the song of success. I also upped the output by ignoring the hoist used to place shells in the machine and by using, in defiance of the rule, the measuring gauge while the shells were turning.

At 15¢ cents per shell I achieved a maximum of 15 an hour with a daily pay ranging between $14 and $18. Only one among the other seven wavers ever soared to such heights and he was on the night shift.

Occasionally wear and tear made it imperative that belts be changed or adjusted and it was not by accident that the dour machinist to whom I have referred made haste slowly when I sought his assistance. On arrival his insulting language was beyond compare. "You", he thundered, "are in need of a thrashing which I will provide. I will meet you on Dufferin Street at 8 o'clock this evening."

"I'll be there." I answered. "Make no mistake about that."

Outside I awaited the coming of this cyclone, the while other wavers forgot to go home. Fifteen minutes passed and a waver named Motrum said, "He must have gone out the back door."

I re-entered the shop and found the belting expert alone and it didn't seem likely that he planned to keep the appointment he had made. I told him then that teamwork was a must if all concerned aimed to keep the Allies supplied with shells. He agreed and a provocative situation was avoided.

A few days later Mr. Millan, a supervisor from Kingston, approached me and said; "I sure scared the daylights out of that battler from Shelburne. When he told me that he was going to 'beat you to a pulp' my Irish wit impelled me to bid him farewell. Before I had finished I had you portrayed as being the toughest hombre who ever came out of Frontenac county. He had his hat and coat on and was en route to the exit when he first spoke to me. A few seconds later he had his hat and coat off and, upon my word, he was repairing belts. And do ye know," said Mr. Millan, "that we Irish should stick together?"

Both comic and tragic incidents occurred in that large factory. A male operator lost a hand when he tried to use the gauge on a revolving shell and Mr. Yellowley issued an order that shells in motion must not be measured. One waver disobeyed the edict and lost a hand. Another operator lost four fingers.

I declined to abide by the ruling because it would have reduced the output. We were working to the twenty-thousandth part of an inch and, thereof, it will be seen that the margin between high and low was extremely narrow. I turned out thousands of shells without incurring a mishap.

With that contract completed the Russell Works got another for 80 pound shells but a layoff occurred to enable workmen to install new machines. During that lapse I secured employment with the Hepburn Machine Company as a waver on light shells but that sojourn lasted only three nights.

During the first two nights I collaborated with machinists in bringing the machines up to highest specifications and when that task was completed I earned $28.60 in ten hours. The result was electrifying, and especially so in view of the fact that no one else had reaped more than six dollars a day.

The foreman, named Harrison, fired me on the spot and when I went to the head office for my cheque Mr. Hepburn asked me why I had terminated relations with the firm. I handed him the slip and replied, "It has been my firm conviction that those of us who are engaged in munitions work should be concerned about swift and flawless production. That is the faith I have tried to keep. Your shop has been operating at a snail's pace because the foreman and the operators don't want you to reduce piece-work stipends. I would wager you the money I made last night that I can perform every operation on a shell in much faster time than any of the so-called specialists."

Mr. Hepburn replied, "That experiment will be made", but I declined, the while I pointed out that the contract didn't demand enough shells to maintain my interest.

As I left the factory, the foreman met me outside and verbally berated me for ringing that 'gong'. He also threatened to assault me but I brushed him aside and a few minutes later he was dismissed by the firm.

At loose ends, I secured employment in the Otto Higel Piano Works where I became an inspector on player piano actions. Under the piece work system in that remarkable setting I amassed the amazing total of $19 for my last two weeks' toil of 110 hours. Thereof, I resigned and eventually returned to the Russell Works where I averaged about $15 a day on the wavers. I also established an untouchable record when I turned out, at 12¢ each, 160 shells one day and earned $19.20.

While I was toiling at the Otto Higel works I had taken time out one night to attend an OHA senior hockey game which featured the Toronto Dentals, Allan Cup holders, against a winless St. Patrick's club team in the Mutual Street Gardens. Very few fans were present; only the Dentals were on the ice and it didn't appear likely that a contest would be staged.

Eventually, I saw W.A. Hewitt, secretary of the OHA, in conference with the referee, Harvey Sproule, and then along the aisle came Jerry Coughlin, my former Haileybury teammate who was a member of the Toronto Arena professionals. The late George O'Donoghue, manager and coach of the St. Patrick's team, talked briefly to Coughlin who, much to my amazement, pointed me out in the crowd.

O'Donoghue then ascended the steps and spoke somewhat as follows, "I hear that you have played hockey. We are faced with a serious problem in that we have only five players and will have to default the game and retire under those circumstances. Would you be kind enough to fill the breach?"

I replied "I would like to help you but I haven't been a hockey competitor since 1915, my skates are at home, I am not in condition and I would be more of a hindrance than a help."

"We'll take that chance", said O'Donoghue, "and you can go through the motions."

Via taxi I rushed to get my skates and when I appeared on the ice Ruby Millan of Kingston and the late Willard 'Bill' Box, one of the fastest skaters I have ever seen, expressed a bit of sympathy. I explained that all I meant to do was to prevent the forfeiture of the St. Patrick's 'franchise'.

I was aligned on defence with Bill Adams, whose brother Jack is well known to all followers of hockey. Bill was also a brilliant player but was not concerned about becoming a professional. I was truly sorry for Adams who had to be paired with me.

During the opening period I made several rushes and on each occasion passed the puck to one of my teammates, none of whom I had ever seen previous to that night. Came the resting interval and O'Donoghue, who had called me aside, said, "Don't pass the puck to any of those forwards. It is strictly a waste of time."

I accepted that advice and through a bit of good fortune I scored twice during the middle session. It was also in that period that I bodychecked the onrushing Bill Box who flew through the air and became entangled in the net. Laughingly, we extricated him but fun turned to gloom when the discovery was made that that brilliant competitor was very badly hurt.

Owing to his excessive speed, I was bowled over when I 'hipped' him but the point of contact had willed unto a fine friend, instantaneous appendicitis. Willard was rushed to hospital with a ruptured appendix but he made such a fast and remarkable recovery that he returned to action the same season.

Late in the game I was charged by Jimmy Steward, a small leftwinger from Kingston, and when he fell I was handed a minor penalty by referee Lew Brown. At that stage St. Pats were leading 5-4 but during my absence "Rube" Millan engineered two successive scoring attacks. I moved to centre on my return and hit the twine a fraction of a second after time ran out.

"You have surprised me", said O'Donoghue as I entered the dressing room."

"I have surprised myself even more," I retorted, "but I rather imagine that those boys from Kingston – Goalkeeper Charlie Stewart, Jimmy Steward, "Rube" Millan and, indirectly, Bill Box – didn't desire to make me look foolish."

In my next start I wasn't so fortunate and I almost lost my life when the late Hughey Fox, playing defence for the Crescents, bodychecked me just below the left hip and willed unto me phlebitis. I finished the game but on Christmas Eve I suddenly collapsed when at dinner and a hurry-up call brought the famous Dr. Charles Hair to the rescue.

That accident occurred fort-five years before this account is being written but the hip has weathered all storms encountered down that long and arduous trail in which I played hockey, lacrosse and football and refereed 2,864 hockey games, 1,187 of them in the National League.

Following recovery I rejoined the St. Patrick's team and participated in the remaining scheduled games. I was offered a contract with the Toronto Arenas of the NHL but rejected it. Those were years, you know, when stipends were ridiculously small.

The "Meteor", who was Willard Box, would have been a sensation in the NHL of any era but the highest offer ever made to him was $900 for the last half of the 1917-18 campaign. He was then a student at the Dental College and he wavered a bit before he cast the die that would keep him always in the amateur fold.

In this era of dizzy salaries the beneficiaries would be surprised to learn that in 1917-18, Toronto Arena club stipends ranged between $400 and $1,200. The late Corbett Dennenay, who drew the $400, was colorful, shifty and fast and when he demanded higher pay the late Charlie Querrie, team manager, offered him a raise of $200 provided that in a match race once around the ice surface he would be returned the winner.

For no plausible reason I was called upon to 'referee' and to the amazement of all concerned the late Reg Noble turned the sprint into a shambles and also won the money prize. In that denouement, the management donated $200 to the speedster who had been expected to prevail.

During the summer months of 1918 I was again a waver in the Russell Works but in September the contract was concluded and with the 'First Great War' moving to its close the making of munitions was halted. Jobs and positions were very scarce so in that dilemma my wife suggested that I should try to get employment as a sports writer.

Editor's Note: Thus started Mike Rodden's newspaper career.

To conclude this part of Rodden's life we will reprint the last portion of an unattributed item, entitled, *"A Mattawa and Canadian Sports Legend"*, which describes Mike's marriage to Millie and moves briskly through the rest of their lives together.

In August 1915, the Roddens committed themselves to each other. Millie boarded a train to visit friends in Montreal and instead, scurried north to Cochrane to marry Michael. At the time, Michael was a clerk for the Trans-Continental Railroad and had sent Millie $50, a whole month's pay, to make the trip.

After stopping to see her friends in Montreal, Millie returned to her parent's home, her new status as Mrs. Rodden a well kept secret. Only several months later did she tell her unamused parents of the marriage.

Michael was a Roman Catholic and Millie was a Protestant and in Mr. Wormwith's opinion mixed marriages were frowned upon and besides, Michael would never make anything of himself.

Michael ignored the Wormwiths and went out to prove himself.

After working in Kingston making shells for the war effort, Mike and Millie moved to Toronto where Mike went to work making 300 pound munitions, but the war was nearing an end.

It was Millie who convinced her husband to to try his hand at sports writing, and in 1918 he became the assistant sports editor for The Toronto Globe. He then became sports editor in 1928. Mike left The Globe for a short time during the Second World War when he returned to munitions work. He also took a job during the war as a fire ranger and game warden, a job he had done during his summers at college.

While in Toronto, Mike coached football teams to twenty different titles including coaching the old Hamilton Tigers to two Grey Cups in 1928 and 1929. But because there was little money in coaching he turned to refereeing hockey by chance. He officiated his first game as a favour to his brother, a rink manager.

> "The referee for a girls' game didn't show up and I
> filled in. That's how it all got started. That's got to
> be something for the book", he said.

While working for The Globe, and coaching football, Michael refereed several games for the Ontario Hockey Association, then moved to the senior leagues. and later refereed in the National Hockey League for 13 years. "I refereed a total of 2,864," he said in an interview at age 82, "and what happened to me shouldn't happen to anyone."

He was refereeing amateur hockey in the days when referees had to dodge lumber, knives, fists and bodychecks thrown by players and fans.

Mike was also a well-respected judge of hockey talent. He personally recommended 32 players who achieved 'star' status in the NHL, such notables are Nels Stewart, Babe Siebert, 'Shorty' Horne, 'Toe' Blake, 'Butch' Keeling and 'Hap' Emms.

He left the Toronto Globe in 1936 and moved to Kingston in 1944 where he became the sports editor of The Whig Standard.

In 1962 Michael was elected to the Canadian Hockey Hall of Fame and in 1964 to the Football Hall of Fame. He was the first person to be elected to both Halls of Fame.

By his side at all times was his wife Millie and sons William and Richard. They were his inspiration.

Michael excelled in everything he competed in, coached or refereed. And besides his hockey, football and editorial feats, Michael chalked up records in canoeing, boxing and ten-pin bowling.

Blessed with an uncanny memory, Mike chuckled about how many times he's been declared dead. "At last count," said Mike in an interview with The Whig Standard on his 60th wedding anniversary, "I must have been reported dead on three occasions. I think that must be a record for me, too."

Michael J. Rodden entered the third and greatest Hall of Fame on January 11th, 1978.

ADDENDUM I

Editor's note - The final segment in Mike Rodden's autobiography was titled "Northland Characters" and in it he returns to the land of his birth to write about some folks who impressed him during his formative years. Herewith a shortened edition of that final chapter in Mike's 450 odd page life story.

Northland Characters

In all mining towns there are extraordinary men. Jack Munro of Butte, Montana, for instance, leaped from obscurity into brief fame when he went four rounds against Jim Jeffries, the world's heavyweight boxing champion who was on tour. Jeffries, however, knocked out Munro in the second round in defence of the title, on August 26th, 1904 in San Francisco.

Following other engagements in which he acquitted himself well, Munro joined the trek to Cobalt. Still later he became the mayor of Elk Lake, a silver mining centre. In January of 1910 there came a day when the members of our assessment party in Porcupine heard some one whistling in the woods. Suspecting that it was an SOS call we replied in kind.

About ten minutes later a huge man struggled through the deep snow and found us in a small clearing. He was almost exhausted and when he saw that we were strangers he reviled us in derision and opined that we were "a bunch of smart Alecs with an odd sense of humour."

As he stood on a small hill near the trench we were digging, I, the only one who recognized him, said, "Unless you have improved since Jim Jeffries knocked you out you shouldn't challenge any one to fight." Munro took one scathing glance at me, turned and vanished into the snow-laden forest.

Jack Walsh, a middleweight boxer, never lost a bout in the north. He and his brother Jimmy, a lightweight, might have attracted world-wide attention if they had elected to make professional boxing a career. On one occasion a highly-rated United States middleweight was brought to Cobalt for the express purpose of knocking out Walsh but the latter stopped him in the fourth round.

Tim Daly, better known as the long-time trainer of the Toronto Maple Leaf hockeyists, appeared half a dozen times in a Cobalt ring and years later he jestingly reported that he had "winned only one". This was news to me because I had never seen him lose by knockout or decision.

Jack Lawlor, who never entered a ring, was the greatest of them all. He was a man of few words who never invited trouble but knew the answers. One night in a Cobalt hotel bar room six tough hombres attacked Lawlor and he knocked them all out with as many blows. An Australian heavyweight mittman, named Riley, aiming at a high place in the sun, challenged Lawlor but a mutual friend of both persuaded Riley to desist.

A few mornings later as Lawlor awaited the arrival of Riley in the LaRose mine bunkhouse I carried a message upstairs to Riley that "zero hour" was just around the corner. Riley, taking the hint, caught the southbound afternoon train and returned to his homeland where a warrant for murder awaited him. He had been under sentence of death when he fled to Canada and, thereof, he was eventually hanged.

Major Eddie Holland, who in connection with Lord Robert's son, won the Victoria Cross at the Battle of Modder River during the Boer War, was a jokester beyond compare. On one occasion he entered a Haileybury bar room on search of liquid refreshment, only to find that the bistro was filled to capacity.

Quickly, Holland crossed the street to a hardware store, purchased a stick of dynamite, extracted its contents, substituted sawdust and rushed back to the hotel. Next he loudly proclaimed that he would 'blow the place to bits'.

With excessive speed all in that bistro, except one bartender, fled through doors and windows, the while Holland calmly ordered a glass of Scotch.

Holland, who also employed the dynamite threat in chasing prospectors away from a claim he sought south of Cobalt, returned one dark evening to his Haileybury home, there to find a prowler trying to open a window. Pulling his hat brim down close to his eyes, Holland approached the miscreant and said, "you are working my claim. I had planned to rob this place tonight but I accept you as a partner." His proposal was accepted and they both entered through the open window. Having collected much silverware and other valuables, Holland said, "Search that pantry under the stairs." Unsuspectingly, the hood obeyed instructions and it was then that Holland turned the key in the lock and called in the police.

One night as I sat in the smoker on a southbound Toronto train with Jim Hughes and Barney McInernly, two prospectors who had struck it rich, Holland suddenly appeared at the door and inquired "Has anybody here got a drink? A woman has just fainted in the car ahead."

Gingerly, Barney reached under the seat and brought to light a pint flask which he handed to Holland. The latter unscrewed the top, placed the vial to his lips and, to the amazement of us all, he emptied the flask. Then, wiping his lips, he said, "Every time I see a woman faint it turns me to drink."

Holland, who returned from the Boer War with a gorilla as a pet, once took that prize to an Ottawa bar room and almost frightened the occupants senseless. When the gorilla hopped to the top of the bar those who had been dishing out the potions broke all known records in vacating the premises.

Long after Cobalt had been almost deserted Holland was the post-master in that once hilarious and highly productive silver mining centre.

Golden City, situated at the east side of Porcupine Lake, was a beehive of activity during summer evenings when cosmopolitan crowds assembled in bar rooms, indulged in spirits and told tall tales about minerals in the Yukon; California; Butte, Montana; South Africa and Australia. There the poor mingled with the rich on friendly terms.

The site where Golden City stands was a snow-covered forest when I first saw it late in 1909. But communities sprang up like mushrooms and only months later Golden City, South Porcupine and Pottsville were thriving villages. There were hotels, boarding houses and stopping places in all three, and there were stores galore.

When the great Porcupine fire came roaring out of the west on July 11th, 1911, South Porcupine and Pottsville, on the west side of the lake, were reduced to ashes in approximately half an hour. The inferno swept around the North side of the lake with awe-inspiring speed; scorched Golden City outbuildings, then split into a V, going northeast to destroy Cochrane and directly east where a forest road built under my supervision diverted it and saved the village of Matheson.

That night Golden City hostels and homes were so jammed to the rafters that hundreds slept in tents which had been hastily erected in the vicinity. Small electric bulbs on posts flickered in the darkness and provided guidance for those who sought to drink away their troubles in a main street bar room.

Although I never had imbibed I went to that 'bistro' seeking information and there I met some of the quaintest characters in the North. Many had harrowing tales to tell about narrow escapes from the inferno and one sang, "There never will be as hot a time in this old town again."

One of those present, a sourdough in Yukon days, took me aside and told me the following factual story:

"Like Robert Service did in the Klondike I have seen many sights during the nights I have spent in this here bistro. As a matter of fact I, too, went over the trail of '98. I heard about "Tex" Rickard, too, but I don't know that he done any prospecting. And some of those characters Service wrote about never existed.

"I panned my share of gold dust and so did 'Old Man' Mousseau, who is 81 but must be nearly 90. And I guess you know he escaped by going back through the fire near where Marshall Morrison was burned to death. As a swampman Mousseau has no equal."

"I know Mousseau", I answered, "I talked to him today."

"But", he replied, "I'll bet you never met the Major. It was to this here room that he came one night and he says, says he, "I'm going to treat the 'ouse." He was English, you know, and he had served in India, the Soudan and South Africa.

"Well, o' course there ain't nobody who is in the house and won't take a nip unless he is an idiot and, begging your pardon for the same, I exclude you because you're a fire ranger and you got a job to do. And most fire rangers I have seen don't need to drink to make themselves look insufficient.

"So, as I was saying before you interrupted me, which you didn't, the small English Major pays for the rounds and he takes his share with a gulp and then he says,

'Gentlemen, and I presume you are all gentlemen, I wish to prowpose and drink a towst on this glowrious occasion because I would like you to remember me when I have gone, which should be soon. This is the towst (toast):

Here's to the girl who's mine, all mine,

She drinks and she bets and she smokes cigarettes

And sometimes – God… bless her, she almost forgets. That she's mine, all mine!'

"Then the Major bows like Lord Roberts or "Little Bobs", he clicks his heels and he marches out into the night. Some of us wonder what this is all about, so we go out and the Major is standing near that light post a block away. When he sees us approaching fast he bows again, takes a revolver from his pocket and shoots himself dead. So I guess he went from there to meet that girl who drinks and bets and smokes cigarettes and, God pity her, sometimes forgets."

ADDENDUM 2

Last Words

When I look a long way back to the late 1890's and the early years of this century and recall how I dreamed and hoped that some day I would see the super-stars of hockey, football, lacrosse, boxing and sports in general I can hardly believe that it all came true. It has been a wonderful world and those wonders never cease.

At the age of seventeen, I wrote in fun, an imaginary story which I think was expressive of the mysteries that impelled me to follow certain stars. It was called a "Day's Ramble" and it appeared in the 1909 April edition of the University of Ottawa Review. It was, in part, as follows.

"All day long the busy city was the scene of unceasing traffic. Smiling cabbies, with their dark hansoms and well-groomed horses, went rattling by. Electric cars dashed down the crowded streets while in anxious expectation newsboys called out the latest sensations of the day. It was a revelation to watch those ragged urchins intermingling with the surging mass of humanity, darting here and there with a dexterity known only to city waifs.

Fine ladies in automobiles sped through the parks and over the costly driveways. Far above me rose the lofty buildings of a modern Gotham. The continuous rattle from the elevated railroad, combined with the faint, hollow rumble of the subway, gradually grew monotonous. Everything, in fact, made up an ideal picture of life in a cosmopolitan city.

I was tired and dispirited, as, late into the afternoon, I wandered aimlessly to its outskirts. As I went on, the houses became less elegant and lofty. The scenes of life changed. From the rich man's domain I had entered that of the poor. Now and then, when an automobile, conveying some pleasure party, dashed recklessly along the narrow streets, the inhabitants would gaze in astonishment at that fast receding vehicle.

Yet, for all their outward simplicity, they were happy, far happier, indeed, than were many of those who reaped gold harvests. Sadly, I turned away from that simple scene and turned my tired steps towards the country of the farmer. For a time the noise and tumult kept ringing in my ears, but, gradually, as I left the city far behind it died away in the distance.

The day was well-nigh done when I reached a last resting-place of man. As I lifted the rusted latch and entered the deserted cemetery I felt a sudden awe steal over me. Great tombs of fabulous price, told where the ashes of a Sage or a Rockefeller lay, while simple, wooden crosses bedecked the graves of the poor.

Presidents, generals, soldiers, commoners, all were equal in the grave. Ah! how little that social inequality mattered not for rich and poor, and young and old, as well as the greatest and the most insignificant were all alike in the land of the great unknown. As I gazed in silent meditation at that lonely scene of death, I heard myself repeating the immortal words of Gray;

'The boast of heraldry, the pomp of power
Or all that beauty or that wealth e're gave
Awaits, alike, the inevitable hour,
The paths of glory lead but to the grave.'

When I awoke from my reverie the sun was peeping over the hills and its last rays lit up, in celestial brightness, the western canopy of leisurely drifting clouds. Slowly the sun sank until at length its bright rays shone no more. Softly, out of the gathering darkness floated the happy song of the milk-maid and the hearty laugh of the returning reaper.

Far to the north I could hear the beautiful melody of some master's violin as it wafted gently over the lea. Anon, I heard the tinkling bells in the sheep-fold. Then, as if by magic, the last peal of the Angelus floated across the hills, then died away in the distance. After a time the master ceased to play, the reaper's songs were heard no more and darkness fell upon the land.

Majestically the moon came up behind the clouds and twinkling stars sparkled on the 'Milky Way'. Eerie shadows cast by the tombs fell across that peaceful cemetery. Far away upon the mountains I heard the whip-poor-wills; occasionally an owl, with flapping wings, flitted in the moonlight.

Something seemed to tell me that I had found the answers I had sought. As I turned away in sadness I recited that touching verse from the masterpiece by Gray;

'Yet even these bones from insult to protect

Some frail memorial still erected nigh,

With uncouth rhymes and shapeless sculptures decked

Implores the passing tribute of a sigh.' "

In this evening of my life, which was prolonged when brilliant Dr. Pearson removed my cancer-stricken left lung in August, 1960, in the Toronto General Hospital, I thank God who did spare me after I had abandoned hope.

During my long career thousands of athletes have answered the "Last Call". Many of them were personal friends and a lot of them had played under my coaching commands.

In summer holidays I go to Bill Phillips' beautiful summer camp near Thessalon or to Moose Head Lodge at Lake Champlain near Mattawa where memories of youthful days are still a verdant green. Both camps are located in scenic grandeur and my wife and I rate them above all others we have seen.

Bill Phillips and his charming wife have always made us welcome and the same can be said of the late Charlie Hisey, Mrs. Edna Hisey and Mr. and Mrs. Norman Mann who made Moose Head Lodge so attractive. Many famous people have found respite from toil in both camps.

The old homestead still stands in Mattawa and Rodden's Hill slopes gently down to Squaw Valley. Ike Tongue operates the large store the Timmins brothers built and he continues to tell tall tales – with extra added – about my fighting prowess; how I ran the Mattawa river rapids on logs when river drivers backed away and how I flashed down the mountain bobsled route when nobody else ever attempted that feat.

That bobsled trail has vanished with the passing of the years. Growing trees erased it and nobody seemed to care. In the nights, however, the bats and the whip-poor-wills flit hither and yon and the "whips", which were seldom seen by man in that away-back-when, have grown so bold that they sit calmly on high trees in the moonlight and even descend upon the mountain roads.

In that town I became a legendary sports figure because I was the only native son who ever earned all-star rating in football or coached seven senior championships-winning teams, two of which captured the Grey Cup. I was also the lone ex-Mattawan ever to officiate in Mann Cup lacrosse finals.

Humor must have its 'innings' and thus I must confess that several years ago I met in Ike Tongue's store a girl I used to know when we were young. "Good heavens", she exclaimed, as she stole a coy glance at my wife, "call out the fire brigade; there'll be trouble in the old town tonight. When Micky was young he beat twenty-eight boys in fistic battles."

"What! Only twenty-eight?" asked Tongue, "Why, I distinctly remember that he lowered a boom on thirty-two but he never caught me because I was a very fast runner and I did no loitering."

My wife was appalled when she heard such badinage but she became appeased when I told her that Ike was an Aesop in manufacturing tales.

It has been a long and trying road but, withal, a thrilling one. When the sun goes down for the last time I hope that each of my friends will say a little prayer for me.

ADDENDUM 3

Editor's note - This autobiography covers the life of Mike Rodden from his birth in 1891 to roughly 1917 when, in essence, he divorced himself from Northern Ontario and while he often visited Mattawa and his friends there, with the exception of a period of time in 1939 and 1942 when he assumed fire ranger's and warden's duties at Algonquin Park and Shining Tree respectively, he lived and worked elsewhere the rest of his life.

In 1937 he was "one of hockey's best known referees" and he was asked to write an article for MacLeans Magazine concerning "the toughest job in the world."

The item appeared in the January 15, 1937 issue and in it Mike describes a number of games and happenings in northern Ontario arenas and involving northern Ontario teams and players.

You may be interested to note the different, more subdued writing style that Rodden used in the late thirties as opposed to that used in his famed "Sports Highways" columns in the Kingston Whig Standard and also in his autobiography.

Photo courtesy of International Hockey Hall of Fame

Herewith then an abridged and edited version of the MacLeans article which Mike entitled –

The Toughest Job in the World

"YOU ROBBER! Kill the referee! Throw him out ! You'll never referee in this town again. You're crooked!

Yes, you've guessed it – it's a hockey crowd yelling at a referee who's made an unpopular decision – the voice of a mob in a frenzy.

Why do sport fans act that way?

I don't know; but I do know that hockey refereeing is the toughest job that sport has to offer. In fact, I'll go even further and say that it's the toughest job in the world.

I can see thousands of eyebrows raised in skepticism at that statement. But I'm sticking to it. I've been through the mill as an official in hockey, lacrosse, football, baseball, softball, wrestling and boxing. I've refereed nearly 1,400 hockey games – Stanley Cup games, Allan Cup, National League, International League, United States Amateur Association games, bush league games. And I'm sticking to my statement: refereeing a hockey game is the toughest job in the world.

All a referee needs in order to be efficient are: (1) knowledge of rules, (2) experience, (3) courage, (4) impartiality, (5) indifference to criticism, (6) ability to make decisions in a fraction of a second, (7) the suavity of a "Philadelphia lawyer," (8) honesty, (9) alertness, (10) diplomacy, (11) the art of ruling firmly yet not tyrannically, (12) ability to handle high-strung athletes.

One would think that veteran players could become capable referees, yet the reverse is the case. Names need not be mentioned, but some of the most helpless officials of all times were athletes who, having become accustomed to applause, could not stand up under verbal criticism when they went out there with a whistle. Their plight was pathetic.

Great referees like Mickey Ion, Cooper Smeaton and the late Lou

Marsh never played professional hockey and very little of any other kind, but they knew how to handle men and were past masters in the art of understanding mob psychology. They made mistakes – everybody does – but they had confidence in their own ability, were enthusiastic and never afraid.

For the most part players are not squawkers, and they sympathize with officials. Some of them will argue, but only in the heat of hostilities. They are all contrition when a tough battle is over.

Bitter Enemies

I made my debut as a hockey referee in a girls' game between Haileybury and Cobalt twenty-one years ago. That was a tough assignment to start with.

It was eight years later, however, before anyone suspected that I might become a professional hockey traffic director, and I must say that Jim Sutherland, Kingston's famous hockey authority, was the man responsible for shunting me into the job.

At that time the Sudbury Wolves, featuring the Green brothers, Alex McKinnon, Bill Duncan, Charlie Langlois, Sam Rothschild and Joe Ironstone, and the Soo Greyhounds, with "Bun" Cook, "Babe" Donnelly, Stan Brown (from North Bay), "Flat" Walsh, Bill Phillips and others of ability, formed a two-team group that was the best of its kind in all the history of hockey.

They were bitter enemies and had a penchant for making life miserable for a referee, so it came about that they couldn't agree on one. They appealed to W. A. Hewitt, the man behind the O.H.A., and he was also in a quandary until Sutherland hove into sight with his bright suggestion that I be given the assignment.

Without giving the matter serious consideration I accepted the appointment, and before I could properly gauge the importance of the situation I was on my way to the Canal City.

I heard that several illustrious referees had fared poorly at the Soo Arena, and naturally I wondered what kind of a reception awaited me. However, I had never been in the Soo before, and as no one there knew me, it looked like an even break.

It wasn't anything of the kind. The great Soo machine destined to win the Allan Cup one year later (1923) was simply not in stride and the Wolves tore them apart to win by 8 to 3. A packed arena saw an unknown referee from Toronto calling the plays in a runaway game and some of them resented such a tragedy.

Later on that evening I strolled into a poolroom owned by the trainer of the Greyhounds, and heard an individual proclaiming that I had sold the game. I was on the point of raising an objection when Bill Phillips, star centre player for the Soo, went into action. Phillips didn't even know that I was a spectator, but he earned my undying gratitude for his sportsmanship.

I ran into many thrilling experiences during the hectic ten-game series between the Wolves and the Hounds, but space does not permit me to enlarge on them. However, the players learned in a hurry that they had to play cleanly, and I was only called on to inflict two major penalties, whereas in the past there had been as many as sixteen fights in one game.

One night I ruled a Sudbury player off for five minutes, and he made an attempt to attack me but was held by George McNamara and "Shorty" Green. He tried to renew the feud at the Algonquin Hotel, but when he detected that I hadn't fainted from alarm he desisted and after that he became one of my best friends.

Then, I remember that after a torrid duel in the Nickel City a spectator gave me notice that I must catch the night train for Toronto or take the consequences. I had intended to leave, but altered my decision. The next day I held a conference with the objector and discovered that he couldn't fight his way out of a paper bag.

In 1924 I had a most interesting experience – one of many of them – at Iroquois Falls. The Greyhounds were the visitors, and it happened that in the first two games of the series they broke even, to the disgust of the home-town fans.

During one boisterous outburst I was made the target of many missiles, and one of them missed my head by inches. Bill Phillips, the imperturbable Soo centre, picked up the "dud" and said, "I don't mind the vegetables, but when they start throwing cutlery, I object." The missile was an open knife.

After the game a traveller from Toronto rapped at the dressingroom door and told me that I was going to be attacked by three men and that the fans were awaiting my arrival outside. The noble trio entered, and all were astounded when I locked the door after admitting them. One of them asked, "Why are you bolting the door?" and I replied, "Because I don't want anybody else to get in, and I don't want any one of you to get out."

We had a most interesting fistic session and each of the trio hit the floor. But my troubles were not over. After the door was opened a heavyweight defenseman on the Iroquois team came barging in and laid a strangle hold on my neck that still is painful, even if only from memory.

Leaving the arena, I was surrounded by belligerent fans, but none of them tried anything drastic. Later that evening, however, a "gentleman" called me a foul name, but, being cross-eyed, he was looking at Bill Phillips when he spoke, and "Thessalon Bill" beat him as badly as Jack Dempsey did Jess Willard at Toledo in 1919.

I went back to Iroquois Falls later that season, was given most cordial treatment and received $300 to referee two games, both of which were lost by the home team.

In the North, the Soo Club paid me a $125 a game, Sudbury $100, Iroquois Falls as high as $150.

I could go on indefinitely with pulse-throbbing reminiscences, but what of that? It would all lead to the same conclusion.

But I repeat that a referee's task presents no bed of roses. He walks by himself. He is not even permitted to travel on the same train as the players, nor stay at the same hotel. He's a kind of an outcast who is never right, and he gets neither sympathy nor support from the club heads or the fans.

Despite all the clamor ever raised, the hockey referee is honest. He has to be to retain his position. He is always on the "spot." Just one bad game may cost him his employment. He is not under contract like a baseball umpire; he is a lone wolf in his profession.

There is however, a definite need for improvement in the status of the hockey referee. If hockey is to live, referees will have to be accorded more support and protection than is the case today. Professional baseball magnates learned this lesson long ago, and thus paved the way for better sportsmanship and more proficient playing. In organized baseball the umpire's word is law. If he is found inefficient he is dismissed, but if he is capable he works in all cities despite protests made by the most powerful organizations or managements in the various leagues. The same should be true of hockey."

ADDENDUM 4

This postcard photograph dates back to between 1885 and 1900 and shows the heart of Mattawa of that time period. The building on the far left is the Mattawa General Hospital, the 25 bed edition, which was built in 1885 and burned down 16 years later. Mattawa hospitals have been burned out three times. The fourth edition stands on the same site.

The next building is the Sacristy and St. Anne's Church which was also destroyed in a conflagration and rebuilt on the same spot.

The next two buildings were the Priest's House and St. Anne's School. Where the school stood is now a playground for the present St. Anne's which is a block away from Second Street on which these buildings fronted.

The big barracks-like edifice on the shoreline was the Catholic Women's League Hall which was used as a military barracks when necessary. It was torn down and is now an empty lot.

Photo courtesy Dana Rodden

Same site 1998

The house fronting on the Mattawa River was the Frank McCracken residence.

The photograph was labelled "Boulevard Des O'Blats" referring to the Oblate Fathers Order which ran the Church and School.

Thanks to Annie Lamont, Marjorie Wall and the Mattawa & District Museum for the above information.

An Historical Note or Two

At the regular meeting of the Mattawa Town Council of Monday, April 9th, 1979 in the Council Chambers, the following motion was moved, seconded, and passed –

"Motion No. 79-83: moved by Salem Turcotte, seconded by Normie Mann:

Be it resolved that the Corporation Town of Mattawa hereby change the name of the Mattawa Community Centre to read in Memory of Mr. Mike Rodden who was a very famous man born in

Photo Peter J. Handley

Mattawa, from this date on it will be known as the Mike Rodden Arena and Community Centre."

The Mattawa Town Council of the time was made up of Mayor Mel Edwards and Councillors Normie Mann, Annie Lamont, Fred Bangs, Paul Swindle, Marjorie Wall and Salem Turcotte.

Mike in old age

ADDENDUM 5

Good Bye

Jim Coleman worked for Southam Press for many years and his columns were syndicated across Canada. He was awarded the Order of Canada and is a member of the Canadian News Hall of Fame, the Canadian Sports Hall of Fame, the Canadian Racing Hall of Fame, the Hockey Hall of Fame (Media Section), and the Canadian Football Hall of Fame (Media Segment).

During Coleman's long career covering sports, he had a stint with The Toronto Globe and Mail, the newspaper where Mike Rodden started his writing career.

On Rodden's death in 1978 Coleman was moved to write the following obituary which was printed in Southam Newspapers of January 13th, among other papers. It is a good way to end this volume, I do believe.

"Michael J. Rodden – usually identified by his colleagues in the public prints as 'Dom Miguel' – was a Canadian sports editor of the

Photo courtesy Queen's University Archives

ANENT MICHAEL J.

old school. Also, he was one hell of an entertaining public character; colorful, controversial and monumentally irascible.

There were few of his contemporaries left to remember Mike when he died Wednesday at the age of 87. But, those survivors can attest to the fact that his nickname 'Dom Miguel,' was appropriate. With his wavy grey hair, his acquiline profile and his imperious bearing when officiating an NHL hockey game or coaching a Grey Cup football contender, Rodden certainly resembled an autocratic Castilian sea lord.

Mike's passing evokes memories of one of the most inglorious eras in the history of Canadian journalism. Today's newspapermen find it difficult to understand how oldtime sports editors like Mike Rodden managed to moonlight as NHL referees, racetrack officials and coaches of some of our most notable athletic teams.

The fact is that some newspaper publishers – particularly in Toronto and Montreal – were such cheapskates that they paid only barely liveable wages to sports writers. Those publishers not only condoned moonlighting, but tacitly, they encouraged their sports editors to take outside jobs to augment their incomes. Thus, the penny-pinching publishers salved their own consciences.

Rodden's salary was probably never more than $50 per week when he was sports editor of The Toronto Globe between 1928 and 1936. However, he was paid $50 per game as one of the regular referees in the NHL. And, undoubtedly, he received an annual honorarium for coaching Queen's University, the Hamilton Tigers and many other Canadian champion football teams.

Lou Marsh, sports editor of The Toronto Star, also was a senior NHL referee for many years and he and Rodden were internationally respected boxing referees. Frank Calder, the president of the NHL, was a former sports editor of The Montreal Herald and he hired newspapermen as officials. Bobby Hewitson, a sports editor for The Toronto Telegram, was another NHL referee for many years and, along with Marsh and

224

Rodden, he became a member of the Hockey Hall of Fame.

Elmer Ferguson, who succeeded Calder as sports editor of the Montreal Herald, acknowledged cheerfully that he had so many outside jobs in the late twenties that he used his Montreal Herald salary ($45 per week) to pay a chauffeur who drove him around in his big Cadillac. Lord Atholstan, who owned the newspaper, fondly regarded Fergy as a financial genius.

To the Canadian sports public from coast to coast Mike Rodden certainly was the best known Canadian sports editor of his Toronto era. The management of The Toronto Star still perpetuates the myth that their Lou Marsh was better known. However, Marsh's fame was, for the most part, confined to eastern Canadian cities. Dom Miguel Rodden not only was famous in the east, due to his numerous national successes as a football coach, his name was also a household word in western Canada where the football fanatics viewed eastern teams with envy which verged on loathing.

I didn't meet Dom Miguel personally until he was rather close to senior citizenship and he was presiding rather grumpily over the sports department of The Kingston Whig-Standard. But, I was enchanted by his gift of total recall when I asked him about oldtime athletes or sporting events of his years as a competitor, coach and referee. He was amazing.

Mike's stories of his own major role in the sporting incidents of his era certainly never lost anything in the telling. He spoke proudly and dogmatically, sticking out his chin to emphasize his declarations. If Mike had a harmless tendency to leave his listeners with the impression he was a champion, then I, for one, am prepared to believe that, by gawd, he was indeed the champion!

Michael J. Rodden was an *authentic* Canadian character."

– 30 –

ADDENDUM 6
Yesterday, Today & Tomorrow

Mattawa is still a quietly picturesque little town nestled between the arms of the Ottawa and Mattawa Rivers; the White railway bridge still crosses the Ottawa just at the junction and these days it is seeing extra duty as it conveys the Timber Train on its way to Temiskaming, Quebec. The Timber Train is an example of a growing Mattawa economy based on ecology and history. It is dubbed "a unique rail excursion through history and nature along the picturesque Ottawa River Valley." The fall colour as seen from the old "Moccasin Line" tracks is truly spectacular.

The Old Rodden homestead still stands at the corner of Fifth and Brydges although there have been many changes to the original structure. Rodden's Hill, now Fifth Street, is still there and you can see how it would provide a thrilling slide back at the turn of the century.

Ike Tongue's store, an old red brick structure which was originally the Redmond Building, still stands on Main Street and lawyer Peter Rutland has his offices there. It is less than a stone's throw from the Mattawa River. The streets are still narrow, the Main Street Bridge is still there and many of the old homes continue to house the descendants of Mike's contemporaries.

Marjorie Wall, who was a member of the Mattawa Council that named the arena in honour of Rodden, is now treasurer of the Mattawa and District Museum. She gave me a tour of the town on a sparkling, colour bright October day as we tried to track down some folks who might be able to identify some faces in some early nineteen hundred photographs from the Rodden family. We didn't have any luck but we had the great pleasure of meeting 94 year old Mary Decaire, 92 year old Annie Lamont (who was also on town council in 1979), 85 year old Armand Ribout and Irvine Burke.

The old Rodden home at 511 Brydges in Mattawa,
now the home of Guy Tremblay and family

As we drove out of Mattawa we passed by the remains of the Trans Canada Hotel surrounded by orange fencing, the only thing left – the jagged edged hole of the basement. The Hotel, referred to in this volume, burned to the ground through the evening of Tuesday, August 19th, 1997 and the early morning hours of Wednesday the 20th. The smoke could be seen as far away as Rutherglen (25 kilometres). The edifice was constructed in 1899 and, at 98, was one of the oldest buildings in Mattawa. In fact it was a long time historic landmark, a symbol, perhaps, of the old Mattawa, the Mattawa of Mike Rodden. The new symbol could be the multi million dollar Canadian Ecology Centre, which just might well lead the community into the 21st century, building on the firm footing of the rivers and the forests and many of the people described in these pages.

Photo Peter J. Handley